Asymptote expands the boundaries of traditional architectural practice with work that ranges from buildings and urban design to gallery installations and computer-generated environments. The firm, founded in New York in 1989 by Hani Rashid and Lise Anne Couture, draws inspiration from a wide range of sources not traditionally associated with architecture, among them the phenomena of information space, the dynamics and tectonics of sports and sports equipment, and organic systems of transformation. Their projects are equally concerned with change and fluctuating conditions — motion, light, speed, and traversing virtual boundaries — as with new forms and generative processes and new types of building systems.

Designed and written by the partners, *Asymptote: Flux* documents projects from 1996 to 2001, including commissions as diverse as a virtual reality trading floor for the New York Stock Exchange; the A3 furniture system for Knoll; the Fluxspace installations at the 2000 Venice Biennale and the CCAC in San Francisco; the Guggenheim Virtual Museum; an experimental music theater in Graz, Austria, and the Mercedes-Benz museum in Stuttgart, Germany.

Lise Anne Couture received a Master of Architecture degree from Yale University. She has held appointments at several academic institutions, including the University of Michigan in Ann Arbor; the University of Montreal, the Stadelschule in Frankfurt, Columbia University, Parsons School of Design, and Princeton University. She is currently the William Henry Bishop Visiting Professor of Architecture at Yale University.

Hani Rashid received his Master of Architecture degree from Cranbrook Academy of Art in Michigan. He has taught at numerous universities, including the Royal Danish Academy in Copenhagen, the Berlage Institute in Amsterdam, the Technical University in Vienna, Lund University in Sweden, and Harvard University. He is currently a professor at the Graduate School of Architecture and Urban Planning at Columbia University. Hani Rashid represented the United States at the 2000 Venice Biennale.

Asymptote was a finalist for the National Design Award in Architecture in 2001. The firm's projects have been widely published and exhibited... ...the United States, Europe, and Asia. Works by... ...collections of the Museum of Modern Art in New... ...odern Art, the Solomon R. Guggenheim Museum,... ...the Netherlands Institute of Architecture, and...

HANI RASHID + LISE ANNE COUTURE

ASYMPTOTE**FLUX**

for Tynan

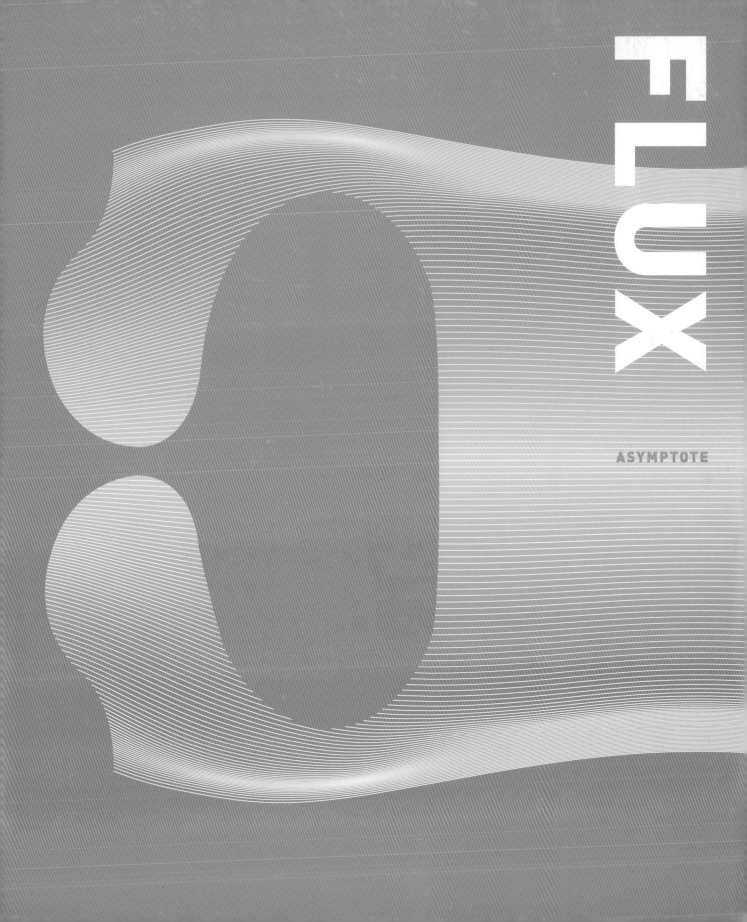

INTRODUCTION

The word Asymptote, defined as two parallel lines that meet at the vanishing point, conveys for us the philosophical underpinnings of our practice. The two lines of the asymptote that constantly approach each other but never touch capture the spirit of an open-ended practice, one that sees each project as part of a much larger body of work, a perpetual work in progress. We understand the object of architecture as being as much about irreconcilability and difference as it is about alignment and convergence. Architecture is a complex field of relationships that results in a dynamic and fluctuating entity. It is significant that the lines of the asymptote, like the many simultaneous pursuits in our architectural practice, do not merge entirely but are rather like trajectories that create an increasingly dense territory between them.

The asymptote, therefore, is an apt reference for a practice that from its very outset was conceived as multi-disciplinary and collaborative. Since its inception we have sought to extend beyond the conventional boundaries of our discipline without limiting ourselves to a singular approach or process. One could say that we operate in a territory between theory and practice. Over the past ten years we have engaged in experimentation with media as various as collage, photographic techniques, digital modeling and imaging, as well as video and multimedia. Our work encompasses the various scales of furniture, interior, building, and urban design, as well as installation art and, most recently, interactive digital environments. As technology has evolved over the course of our practice we have sought to embrace its creative potential while intellectually and architecturally investigating its cultural and spatial implications.

In both our professional and academic research we have been very interested in the potential of an architecture that brings together both virtual and real space. We have aimed to explore the possibilities of virtual architecture in terms of what it might inspire and bring to building in the physical world. The advent of digital technologies has not only provided us with new techniques and processes but also new realms for interaction and the deployment of architecture. Yet virtual architecture and architecture based in the physical world are not necessarily mutually exclusive; our work continues to investigate and explore how one can affect and influence the other.

Experimental and speculative works continue to be an important aspect of our practice. These provide opportunities to conduct research for our various building and digital projects, from the use of new technologies and "intelligent" materials, to issues of contemporary inhabitation and cultural significance. All of these concurrent pursuits typify our drive to tread unknown territories and explore new possibilities for architecture with the aim of creating meaningful and inspired spatial experiences.

HR and LAC

00:00:21:03

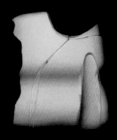

00:00:21:16

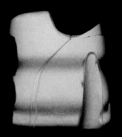

00:00:21:29

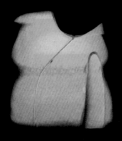

00:00:26:00

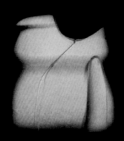

00:00:25:27

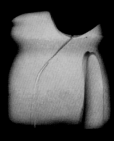

00:00:26:10

6

00:00:35:13

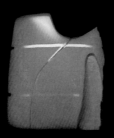

00:00:35:17

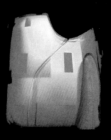

00:00:35:17

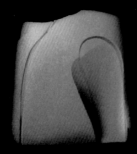

00:00:51:27

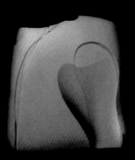

00:00:52:26

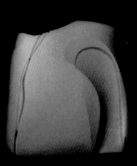

00:00:55:21

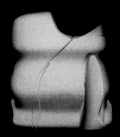

00:00:22:06

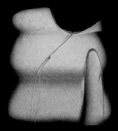

00:00:22:17

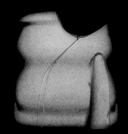

00:00:23:00

00:00:26:29

00:00:34:06

00:00:35:05

00:00:37:07

00:00:38:15

00:00:38:22

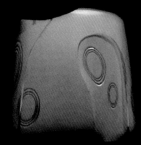

00:01:16:02

00:01:17:04

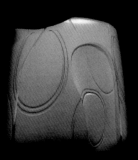

00:01:18:00

I.SCAPE 1.0

Fluxspace 1.0 Installation
CCAC Institute, San Francisco, California

Fluxspace 1.0 was created as a Capp Street Project artist-in-residency work at the California College of Arts and Crafts (CCAC) in San Francisco. The aim of the Fluxspace projects is to blur the distinction between virtual and actual through an exploration of digitally augmented architectural constructs. Fluxspace 1.0 is a full-scale built work in which digital technologies were used in both the design and manifestation of the piece. It is an installation of ambiguous scale whose size lies somewhere between that of large model and small building. Computer modeling was used to derive the three-dimensional form and to create full-size computer-generated templates. The computer's

ability to create a model with a high degree of accuracy, and to output to exacting specifications, afforded the opportunity to create a constructed counterpart at one-to-one scale to the original virtual entity.

The "architectural reality" of the installation was augmented by digitally manipulating the wireframe assemblies and their virtual surfaces. The transformations were then mapped precisely onto the physical objects in the gallery space through the use of video projectors. These "distortions" were then triggered by surface-embedded sensors, sensitive to movement and proximity. Once the sensors were triggered, animations of the distortion of the object

were projected onto the physical piece, creating the effect of a structure in a constant state of mutation and distortion in real time and real space. As one approached this built artifact or passed a hand over its surface, the object would immediately respond by means of its electronic counterpart.

An audio soundtrack derived from the same algorithmic structures deployed to manipulate the form accompanied each physical transformation, thus completing the multidimensional experience.

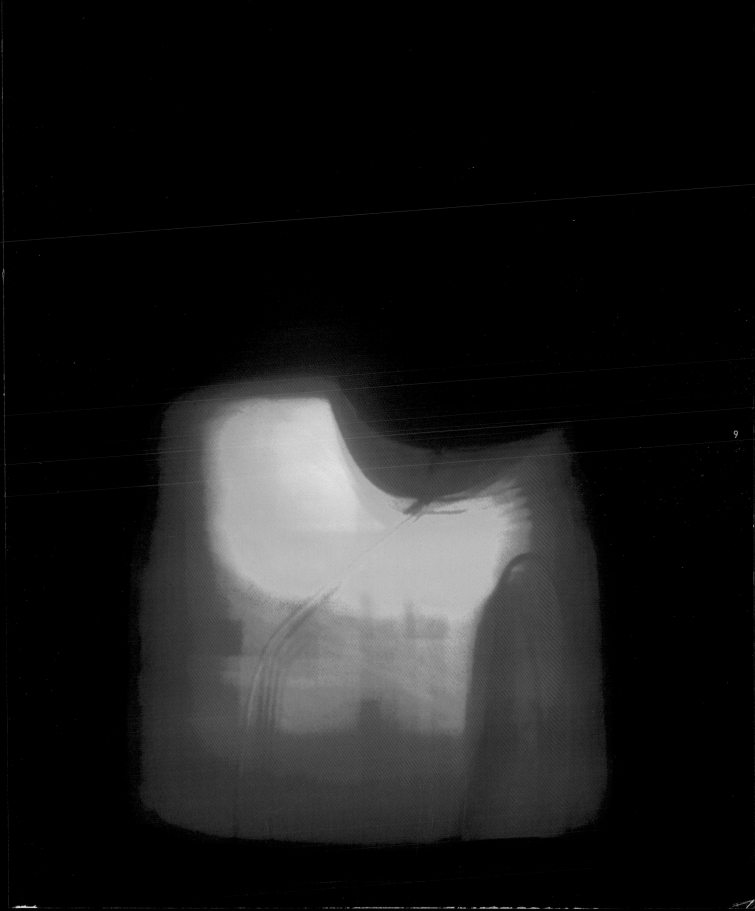

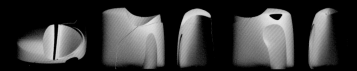

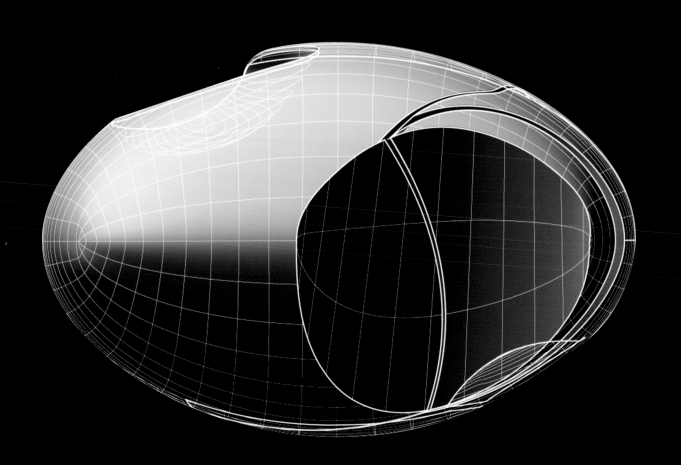

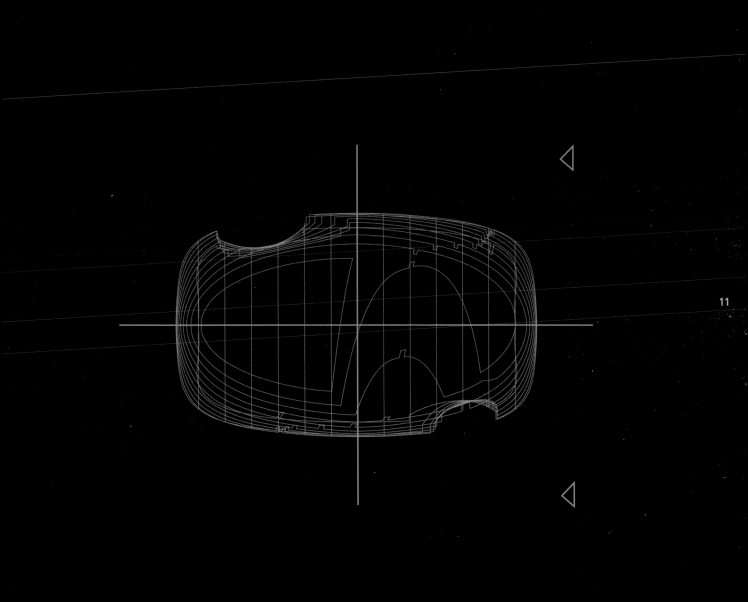

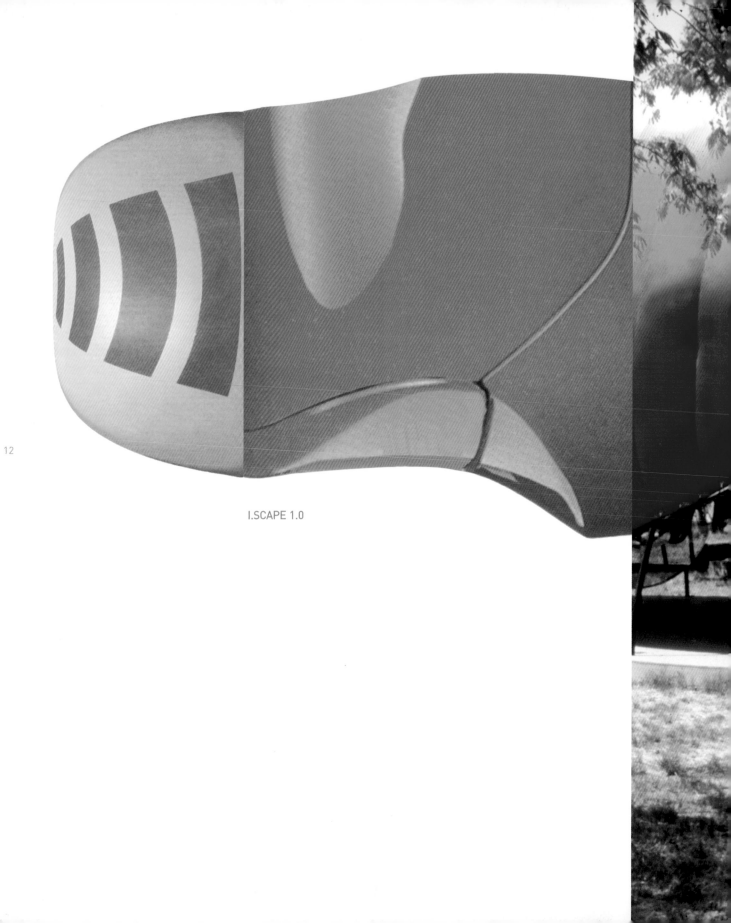

I.SCAPE 1.0

12

Fluxspace 2.0 Pavilion
Venice Biennale, Venice, Italy

Asymptote's involvement at the 2000
Venice Biennale was twofold, comprising
Hani Rashid's participation in the United
States Pavilion and Asymptote's large-
scale, freestanding installation in the
gardens. Both efforts were meant
to contribute to and enlarge the modes
of exhibiting and experiencing
architecture. The projects in the United
States Pavilion were works in progress,
experiments that for the first time

transformed the pavilion into a laboratory.
With these projects there was no need
to mark territory, because the gardens
and pavilions of the Biennale already
provide a well-established cultural venue.
The installation in the gardens sought
to engage an audience including but not
limited to visitors to the Biennale by
providing a simultaneous spatial
experience for a virtual audience.

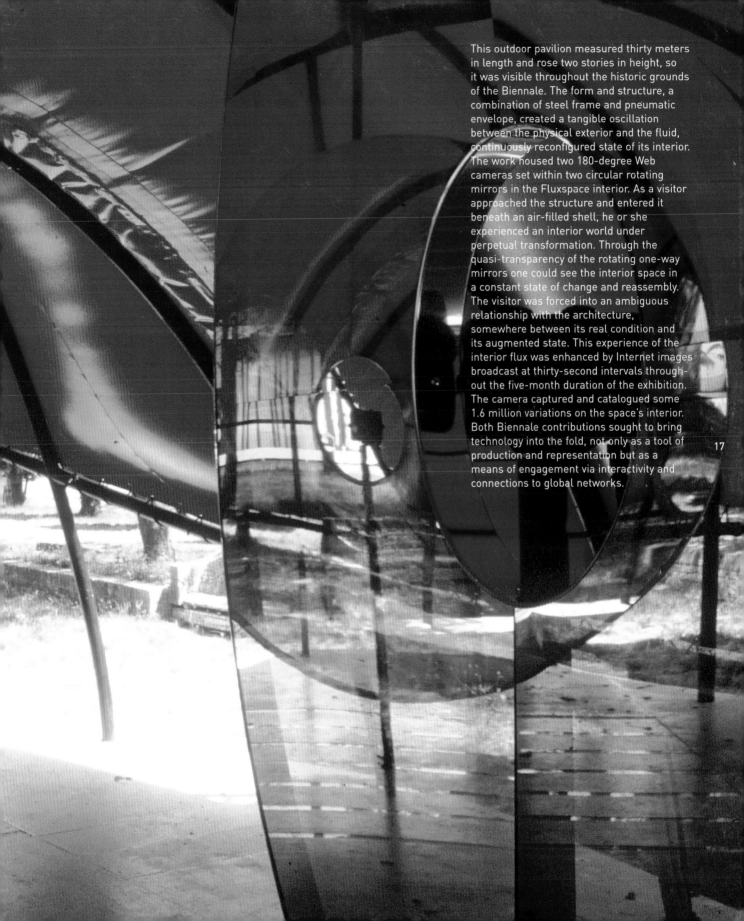

This outdoor pavilion measured thirty meters in length and rose two stories in height, so it was visible throughout the historic grounds of the Biennale. The form and structure, a combination of steel frame and pneumatic envelope, created a tangible oscillation between the physical exterior and the fluid, continuously reconfigured state of its interior. The work housed two 180-degree Web cameras set within two circular rotating mirrors in the Fluxspace interior. As a visitor approached the structure and entered it beneath an air-filled shell, he or she experienced an interior world under perpetual transformation. Through the quasi-transparency of the rotating one-way mirrors one could see the interior space in a constant state of change and reassembly. The visitor was forced into an ambiguous relationship with the architecture, somewhere between its real condition and its augmented state. This experience of the interior flux was enhanced by Internet images broadcast at thirty-second intervals through-out the five-month duration of the exhibition. The camera captured and catalogued some 1.6 million variations on the space's interior. Both Biennale contributions sought to bring technology into the fold, not only as a tool of production and representation but as a means of engagement via interactivity and connections to global networks.

17

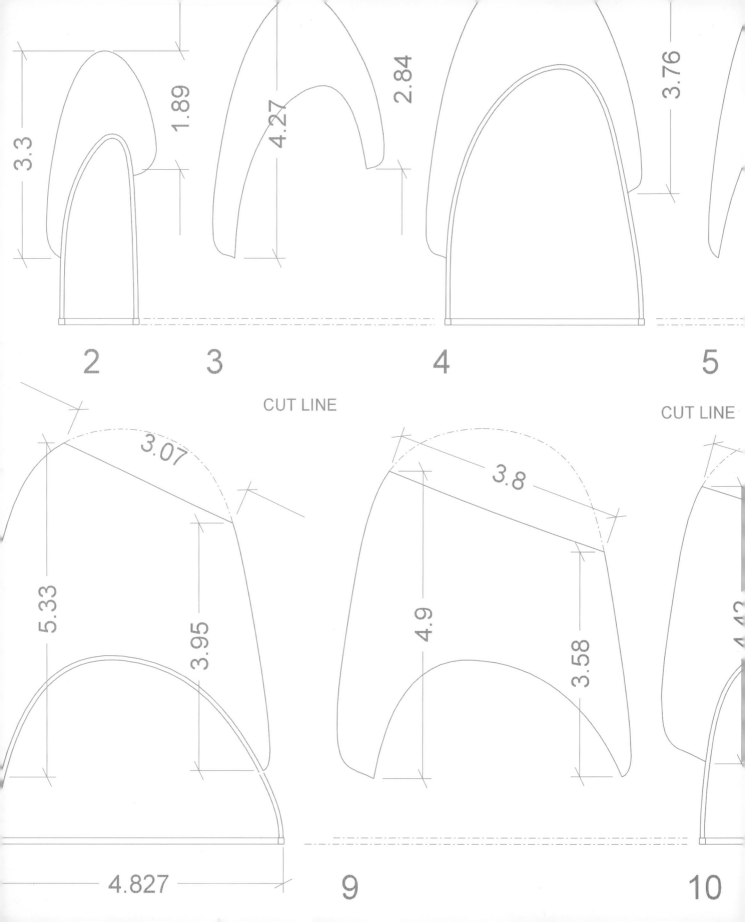

3.3

1.89

4.27

2.84

3.76

2

3

4

5

CUT LINE

CUT LINE

3.07

3.8

5.33

3.95

4.9

3.58

4.827

9

10

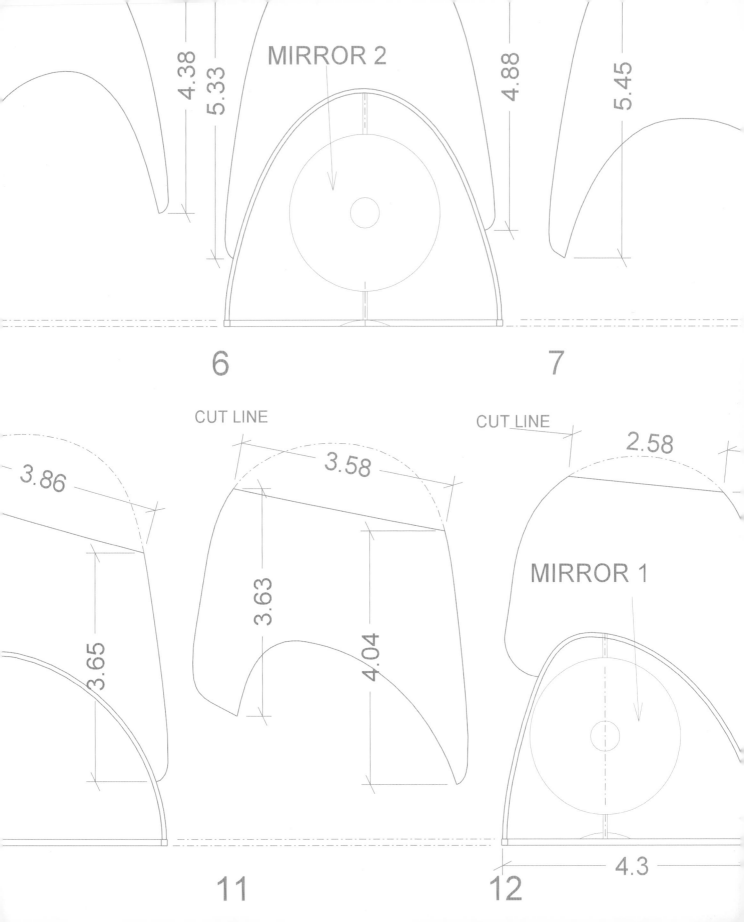

4.38

5.33

MIRROR 2

4.88

5.45

6

7

CUT LINE

3.86

3.58

CUT LINE

2.58

MIRROR 1

3.63

3.65

4.04

11

12

4.3

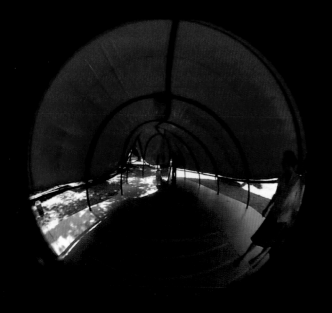

12:00:39

12:14:50

14:14:36

15:30:18

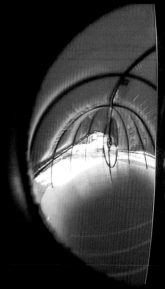

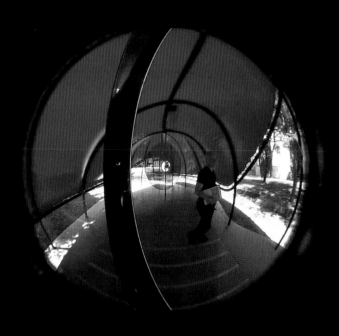

13:05:11

13:51:22

16:22:01

16:59:44

New York Stock Exchange Advanced Trading Floor
New York, New York

Asymptote completed two projects for the New York Stock Exchange (NYSE) in 1999. One is a virtual-reality trading floor displayed on an array of large flat-screen monitors and which enables NYSE personnel to oversee all activity and events on the trading floor. The second project is the design of a new Advanced Command Center located on the actual NYSE trading floor.

The state-of-the-art command center came about as a result of the NYSE's need to update its facilities and accommodate the virtual-exchange model and interface. The command center is also a veritable theater of operations: It can serve as the backdrop to media events staged from the floor of the NYSE and is a means to showcase the exchange's technological advances and capabilities.

A primary element of the architecture is a large backlit surface of curved and tilted blue glass that creates the effect of a liquid backdrop. The structure supporting the glass wall includes horizontal steel posts that also provide data feeds for up to sixty high-resolution, flat-screen monitors as well as the array of nine other screens that display the virtual trading floor. The steel posts also support the flat-screen monitors, creating a floating plane of plug-and-play display panels that can be tiled and synchronized into a variety of arrangements for ultimate flexibility.

The architecture is conceived as a physical analog to the movement and continuous flow of data and information throughout the space of the NYSE. The curvature of the glass and accompanying double-curved work surface, the floating plasma monitors, a large graphic intervention that resembles a digital fresco, and embedded messages boards in the surrounding surfaces create a seemingly seamless and smooth space. The design of this physical intervention on the NYSE trading floor resulted from our experience reconstituting the NYSE in virtual space. The architecture was influenced less by physical surroundings than by an attempt to spatialize the movement of bodies and the flow of data and information.

26

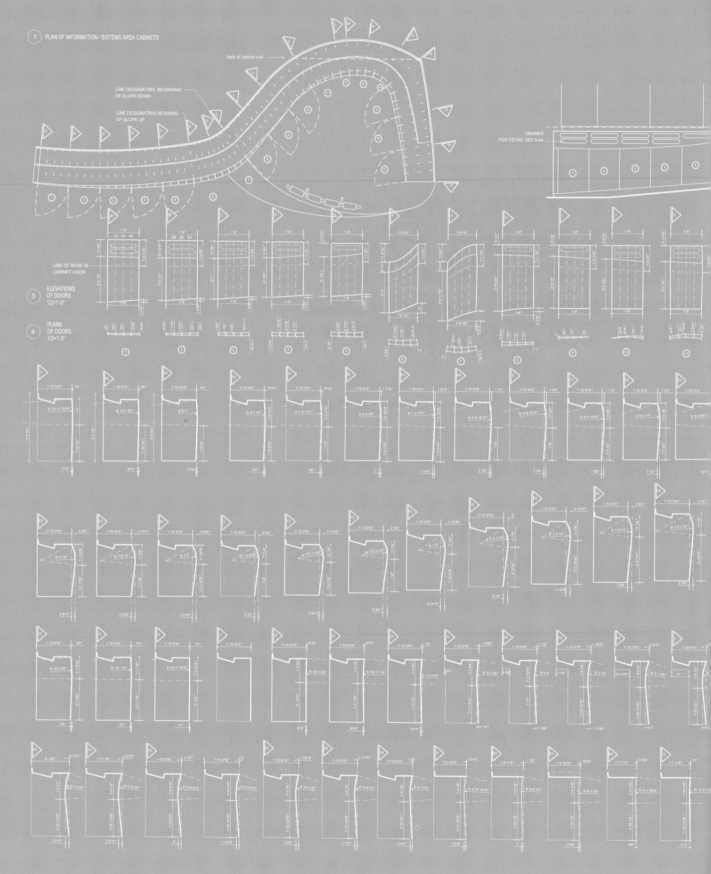

1 PLAN OF INFORMATION / SYSTEMS AREA CABINETS

back of cabinet wall →

LINE DESIGNATING BEGINNING
OF SLOPE DOWN

LINE DESIGNATING BEGINING
OF SLOPE UP

DRAWER
FOR DETAIL SEE 6-A4

LINE OF BEND IN
CABINET DOOR

3 ELEVATIONS
OF DOORS
1/2"=1'-0"

4 PLANS
OF DOORS
1/2"=1'-0"

28

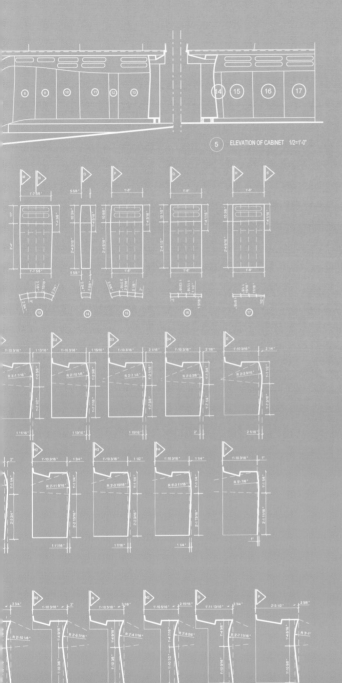

5 ELEVATION OF CABINET 1/2=1'-0"

29

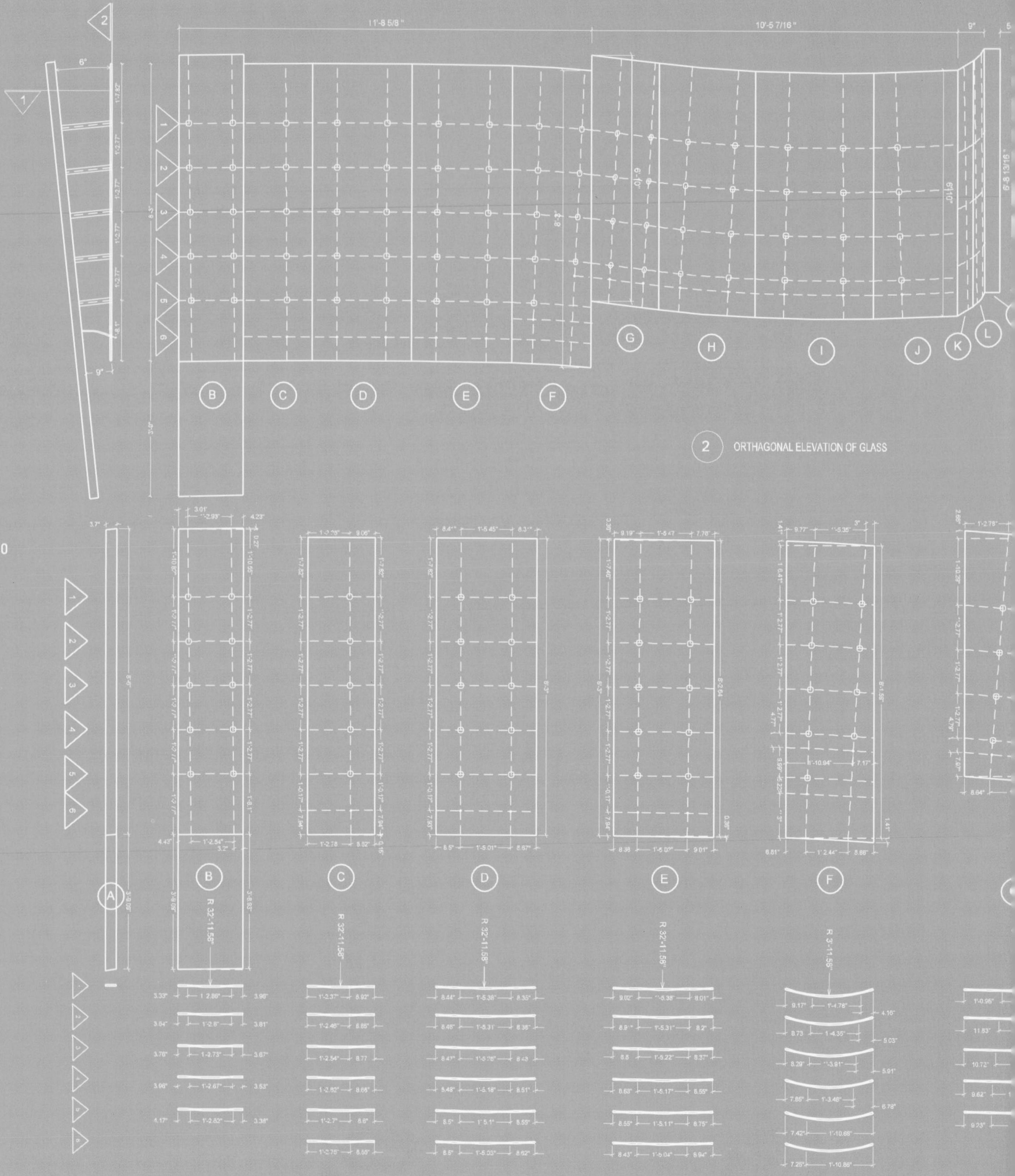

2 ORTHAGONAL ELEVATION OF GLASS

11'-8 5/8"   10'-5 7/16"   9"

B C D E F G H I J K L

A B C D E F

R 32'-11.58"

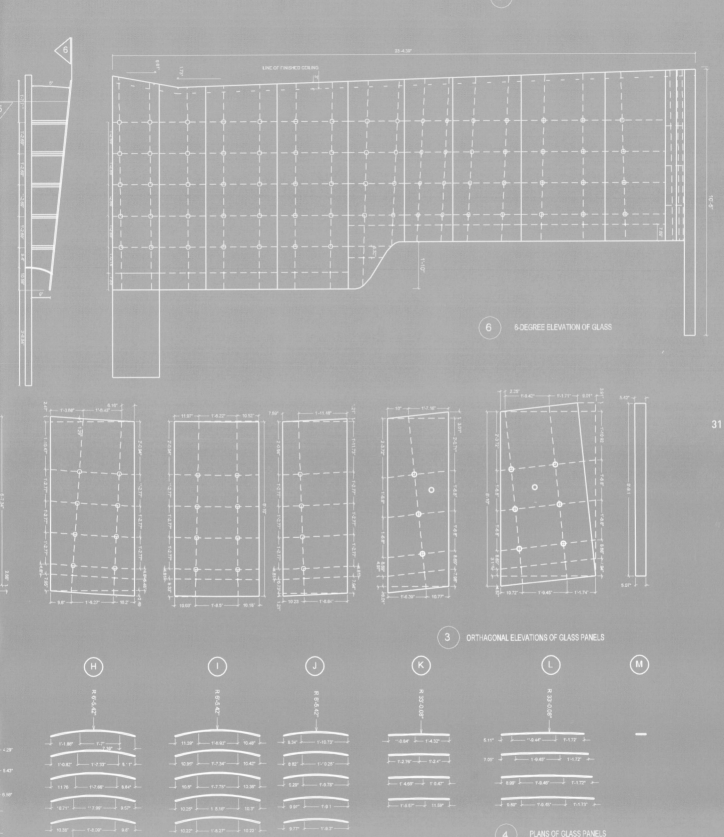

5 6-DEGREE PLAN OF GLASS

6 6-DEGREE ELEVATION OF GLASS

3 ORTHAGONAL ELEVATIONS OF GLASS PANELS

H   I   J   K   L   M

4 PLANS OF GLASS PANELS

31

VORTEX THE NEW YORK STOCK EXCHANGE AND ASYMPTOTE ARCHITECTURE

E AND ASYMPTOTE ARC

VIRTUAL VORTEX

In 1998 the New York Stock Exchange (NYSE) approached Asymptote with an intriguing project. Since the NYSE had been developing a strategy for dealing with the ever-increasing complexity of managing their data and information, they asked Asymptote to develop a virtual environment that would facilitate the reading, correlation, and navigation of massive amounts of information. The NYSE determined that the complexity of real-time information that their staff must contend with on a daily basis required an innovative solution reliant on three-dimensional visualization. As the design for the computer-simulated environment proceeded, it became apparent that there were indeed a number of architectural issues to deal with. Primarily, one had to consider how to navigate through a realm of data. This instigated an approach whereby information is fused with a virtual terrain or landscape using composition, form (tectonics), movement, and the like.

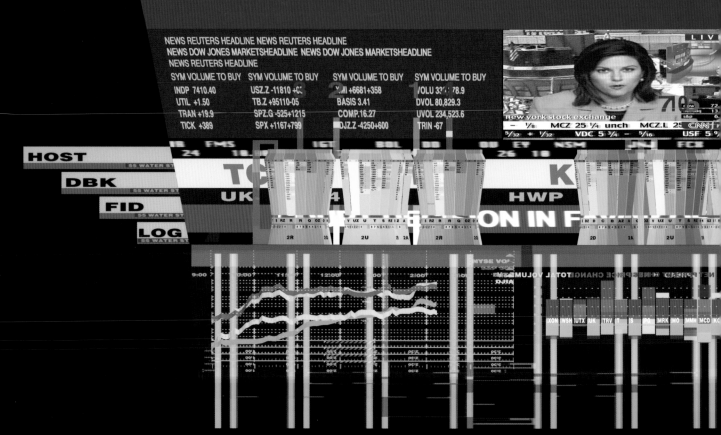

The design of the virtual trading floor (3DTF) began as a reinterpretation and transformation of the existing physical trading environment. The NYSE floor was idealized and refined for eventual virtual deployment. This was accomplished by developing a wireframe model that corresponded to the layout of the "real" trading floor and its constituent elements, their relative placement and geographic location on the floor. The architectural idealization had to provide absolute flexibility; particularly to accommodate the data feeds that would eventually be pro-

grammed into it. The modeling also needed to provide for constant shifts in scale, enhanced levels of detail, and the insertion of numerous other kinetic virtual objects. Thus the actual trading floor had to be reconfigured for several reasons: the model had to function in real time, which produced high technological demands; and an economy of form was necessary to process and animate extremely large quantities of data.

Second, the project took full advantage of opportunities in virtual space to manipu-

late spatial and temporal dimensions. The 3DTF allows one to occupy several virtual spaces, scales, and points of view simultaneously. Captured events can also be instantly replayed alongside real-time events, and the user is able to compress, stretch, distort, or overlap these as required. The importance of the temporal dimension is evident as the inextricable relationship between financial "events" and media news-reporting of cause-and-effect is made transparent. The project posed an interesting opportunity to reconsider the "reality" of the actual

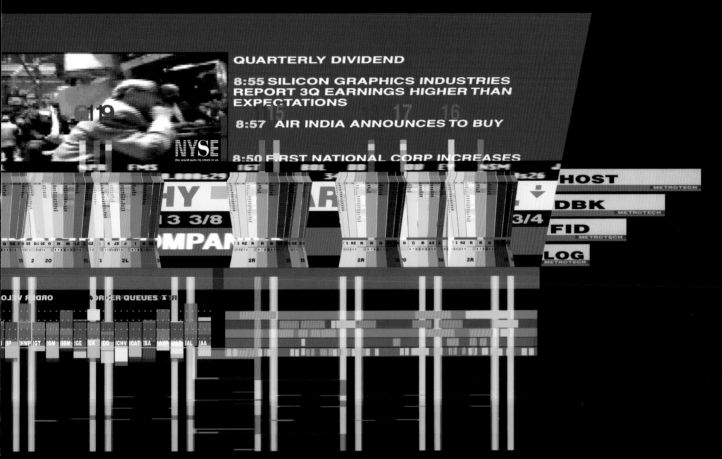

trading floor: Asymptote's 3DTF version of the trading floor, although virtual and not intended to be constructed outside of a computer environment, is effectively a direction for possible future trading environments. The virtual trading floor as designed is both a reflection of the existing environment and a provocation for a new, physically augmented architecture.

The scope of objects and assemblies that comprise the virtual trading floor includes two facilities of computer servers and networks, news and data feeds, and almost limitless data-mining capabilities. All of the information that is relevant to the NYSE and its daily activity of trades and transactions is mapped into this fully navigable multi-dimensional world. Although the virtual-reality environment was initially designed to enable the NYSE to supervise their trading environment, the project has recently evolved to cater to other uses, including a large-scale Internet initiative and a television broadcasting environment. These mutations and elaborations of the project have further architectural implications as the virtual realm slowly usurps the real trading floor as a "place." The fact that the general public will soon be able to navigate a virtual trading floor, check stock news and valuations, make trades, and meander about at will, is unprecedented and begs the question, What actually constitutes an architectural experience and presence? And for those who do inhabit and are familiar with the real trading floor, what new insights into their environment can be attained and how might these alter their understanding of what constitutes architecture?

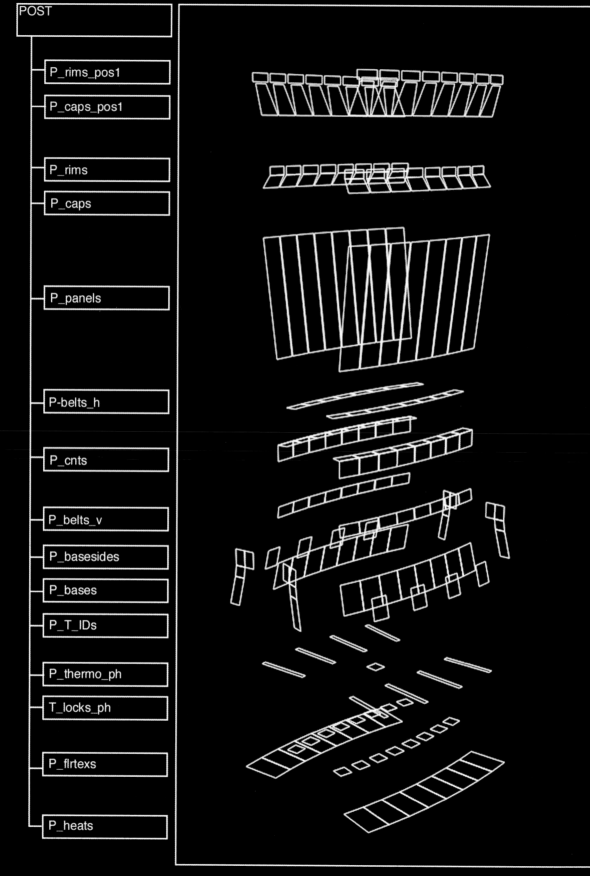

POST

P_rims_pos1

P_caps_pos1

P_rims

P_caps

P_panels

P-belts_h

P_cnts

P_belts_v

P_basesides

P_bases

P_T_IDs

P_thermo_ph

T_locks_ph

P_flrtexs

P_heats

40

GROUPS   WIREFRAME

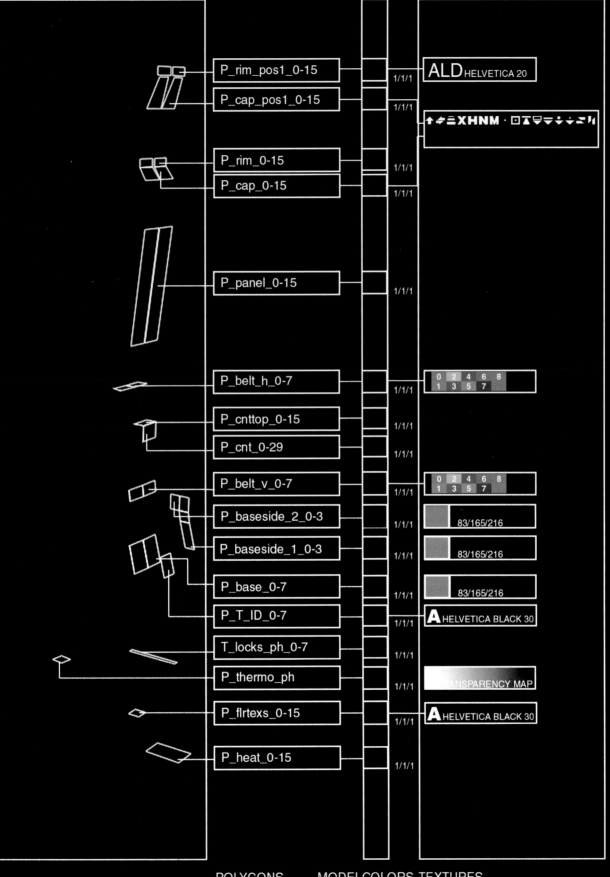

P_rim_pos1_0-15

P_cap_pos1_0-15

ALD HELVETICA 20

P_rim_0-15

P_cap_0-15

P_panel_0-15

P_belt_h_0-7

| 0 | 2 | 4 | 6 | 8 |
| 1 | 3 | 5 | 7 | |

P_cnttop_0-15

P_cnt_0-29

P_belt_v_0-7

| 0 | 2 | 4 | 6 | 8 |
| 1 | 3 | 5 | 7 | |

P_baseside_2_0-3

83/165/216

P_baseside_1_0-3

83/165/216

P_base_0-7

83/165/216

P_T_ID_0-7

A HELVETICA BLACK 30

T_locks_ph_0-7

P_thermo_ph

TRANSPARENCY MAP

P_flrtexs_0-15

A HELVETICA BLACK 30

P_heat_0-15

1/1/1 (repeated beside each row)

POLYGONS   MODELCOLORS TEXTURES

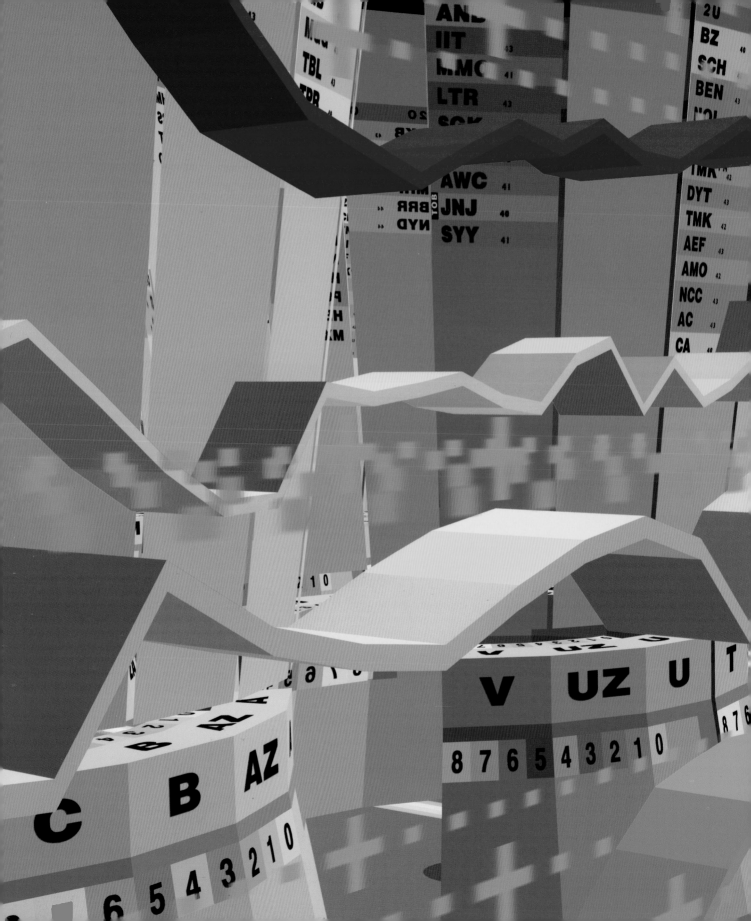

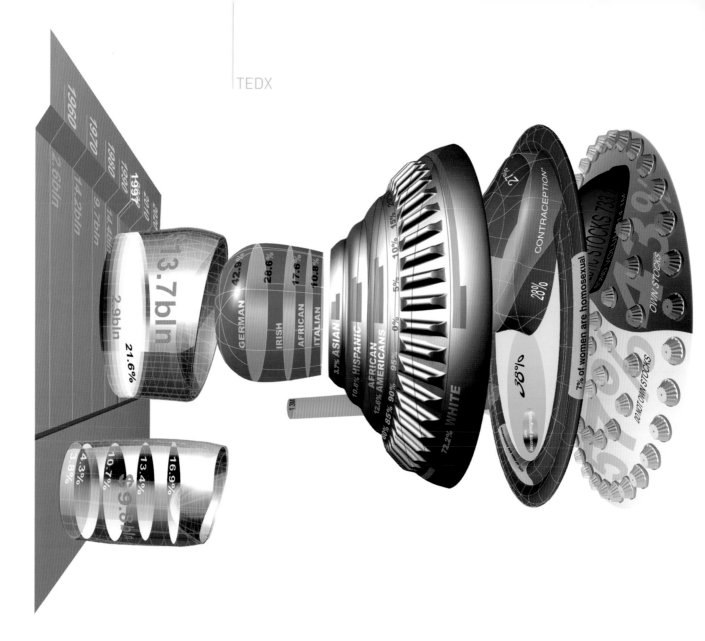

44

These datascapes are part of Asymptote's contribution to a book titled *Understanding USA*, published on the occasion of the 2000 TedX Conference (Technology, Entertainment and Design). This annual event, held in Monterey, California, features a diverse group of speakers from the worlds of technology, entertainment, and design. The goal of the book was to challenge conventional means of representing data, in this case American statistical data. The editors provided each "information architect" contributing to the book with specific sets of data from a wide range of subjects pertaining to America and the American population.

As the content of the book was also to be accessible via an "Understanding USA" Web site, Asymptote chose to explore the potential of three-dimensional graphics to reinterpret the data sets. Rendering the information in navigable three-dimensional entities provided a rich domain for conveying the relationships between different data sets. This approach also allowed for the use of dynamic modeling to represent change in the setting of different variables. The two-dimensional representations in the book were ultimately still frames taken from the three-dimensional models.

Using virtual reality markup language (VRML), Asymptote created eight models intended for deployment on the Internet. Each three-dimensional model can be manipulated and adjusted according to certain criteria. The adjustability and transformative aspects of these data entities allow each subject to be analyzed and scrutinized from different viewpoints. From these different vantage points, one can reference information in a variety of ways. Timelining, for example allows one to make certain adjustments to the data according to varying time periods; or, one can reverse or fast-forward a timeline to see how the datascape alters and trans-

forms. By choosing one element in the data model and adjusting it according to some specific criteria, related items will also be reconfigured and adjusted accordingly. Here various correlations can be made between information that might otherwise be overlooked or misconstrued. This new method of reading, recording, and gathering information creates a much richer and deeper understanding of information than do conventional graphing and charting systems.

The datascapes consist of three main components that make them interactive entities for eventual transmission over the Web. They were initially modeled as rudimentary wireframes and kept "lightweight" in order to be read efficiently despite the bandwidth restrictions of the Internet as the technology exists today. After the design was refined and the models were exported as VRML, various features were attributed to the wireframes, including animation, interactive components, and motion sensors. The models are also texture-mapped to give them tectonic characteristics, including lighting and shading. The updatable, moving texture maps give the datascapes their "live" feedback capability when accessed and manipulated over the Internet. Because the models can be updated continuously, these data entities could remain current indefinitely. Also, as time elapses and new data is incorporated, these entities become valuable as mnemonic containers of information. They are effectively a living record of all of the past data inputs. A record of data captured at different moments in time, from various points of view, would form a very significant means of understanding junctures, milestones, thresholds, and correlations over time.

RACE DATA-OBJECT

SEX AND SEXUALITY DATA-FORM

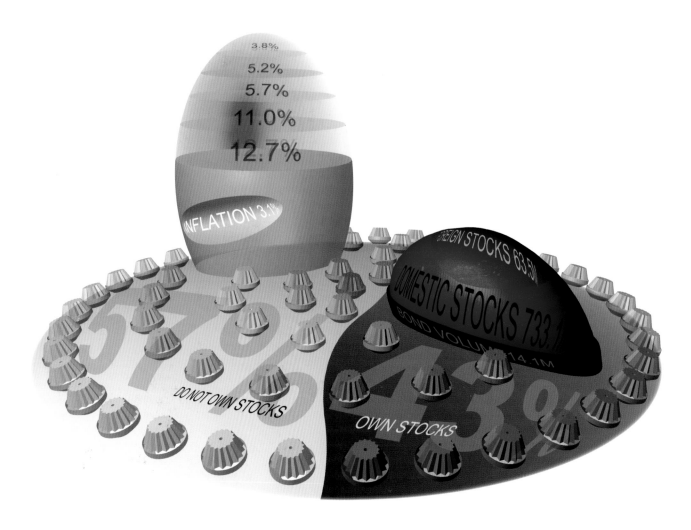

3.8%
5.2%
5.7%
11.0%
12.7%

INFLATION 3.1%

FOREIGN STOCKS 63.5M

DOMESTIC STOCKS 733.1

BOND VOLUME 14.1M

57%

43%

DO NOT OWN STOCKS

OWN STOCKS

STOCKMARKET DATA-TERRAIN

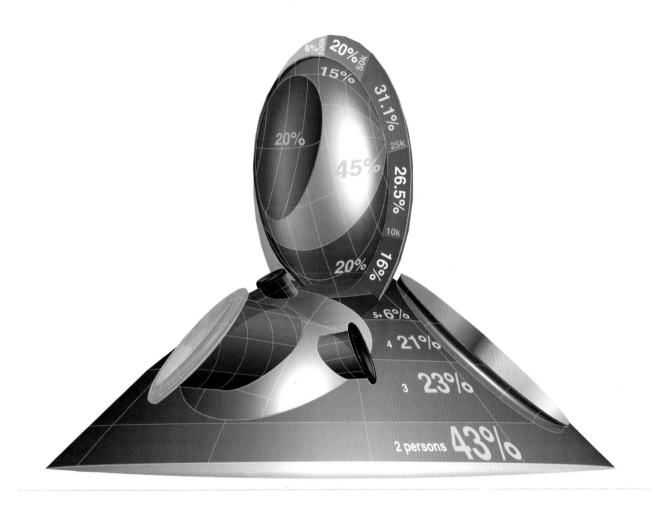

FAMILIES DATA-GADGET

We are in the very early stages of a digital revolution whose direction we will not be certain of for some time, much in the same way that Enlightenment-era architects, theologians, and thinkers did not quite comprehend the profound changes taking place in their own time. Today's digital technologies are having profound effects on many aspects of our contemporary understanding, from the human genome to the mapping of the cosmos. Digital manipulations that use virtual-reality technologies form a major part of this revolution. As architects we are responding in a number of ways, by conceiving of entirely new geometric principles, new methodologies, and entirely novel approaches to representation beyond perspectival geometry.

Virtual architecture is an evolving discipline that results from the convergence of data mapping and simulation, digital form making, information "architecture," and virtual reality constructs and theory. This field of research is being defined by projects and clients that differ greatly from one to another. Conventional architectures tend to be based on permanence and geometric certainty whereas virtual architecture utilizes digital technologies to augment real events, time, and space. In the history of architecture, representation — whether manifest through modeling or other forms of simulation — has always been part of the architect's repertoire of conceptualizing and conceiving space.

Visionaries for their time, Claude-Nicolas Ledoux, Etienne-Louis Boullée, Piranesi, Bruno Taut, and El Lissitzsky are but a few examples of architects whose works can be thought of in today's context as early and important examples of virtual architecture. The Campo Marzio of Piranesi, for example, can be reinterpreted as a data environment in which the buildings and architectures he envisioned each represent an idealized accumulation of "architectonic" information. A similar interpretation could be applied to the proto-surrealist paintings of Hieronymus Bosch and Mathias Grünewald. Artists and architects have always searched for the means to represent utopias, dystopias, visions, possibilities, and actualities. In many ways, virtual architecture has its deep and profound precedents in these histories of visualization and visionary works. The computer has merely extended our ability to visualize and theorize such spatial entities.

Virtual architecture is perhaps best understood as spatiality based on the alteration of reality, on mapping flux, and on the transformable possibilities of geometry within such realms. The commission to design the Virtual New York Stock Exchange (NYSE) necessitated a proposal for a multi-dimensional interactive data environment to be used primarily as a monitoring tool by the NYSE operations group. This project's virtual architecture was based on a data visualization paradigm, where vast amounts of information could be more easily managed through a three-dimensional, manipulable digital interface. It is important to draw a distinction here between virtual architecture and virtual buildings, just as one draws a distinction between architecture and buildings. In virtual architecture the assumption is that spatial, informational, and temporal circumstances provoke experiences and create assemblies that are tangible and plastic. Virtual buildings, on the other hand, tend to be representations of buildings and built space as we already know them to be: for example, a virtual rendition of Le Corbusier's unbuilt Palace of the Soviets complex. This is actually virtual representation, which we tend to call virtual buildings, especially if we can inhabit them in three-dimensional representations. Virtual architecture does not represent or attempt to mimic any aspect of "real" building; rather, it is architecturally significant for entirely different reasons. The Virtual NYSE is not a rendition or re-presentation of the existing facilities: Such a version would have entailed a model with marbled textures on the walls and perhaps even avatars strolling about the floor. That kind of representation ultimately is of little value in a data-driven information environment. The three-dimensional trading floor (3DTF) supplements the main trading floor, allowing users to enter a parallel "reality" and exist in an entirely different place.

The Guggenheim Virtual Museum (GVM) was another commission that had a very unique mandate and purpose. The Solomon R. Guggenheim Museum commissioned the project as an Internet-based museum for the display and deployment of digital art and Internet-produced art, anticipating a future in which new forms of expression will inevitably require new and profoundly different methods of exhibition, collection, and use. This new museum on the Web is not restrained by gravity, traditional notions of movement and viewing, inflexible formal strategies, or the physical limits of real space. The GVM celebrates new possibilities for architecture and experience, such as fluidity, immersion, and replay. For the moment, these criteria and concepts are only possible in cyberspace and through virtual reality; however, the inevitable challenge for architecture is to bring some of these discoveries into "first reality," making them an implicit part of our new built environments in the future. Whereas the GVM is a multi-dimensional digital interface containing "visual" clusters in the form of artist-commissioned works, it also posits a situation in which virtual architecture sits alongside the experience of actual architecture. In order to explore this possibility further in the built environment, Asymptote executed various projects at the 2000 Venice Biennale, including a large-scale installation situated in the Biennale gardens on the historic exhibition grounds. This physical space contained computers and Web cameras that mapped the movement of people and the architecture itself over time. This data was broadcast at a 30-second refresh cycle on the Internet. The resulting physical changes to the actual architecture enacted by Biennale visitors were recorded and viewed throughout the world in real time, which allowed distant visitors to experience architecture in this "virtualized" and mediated condition.

The Venice experiments, and others constructed in various venues, explore the notion of the real in architecture as a blurred condition: that architecture today might be comprehended as a territory located between the real and the virtual. It is important to note that although the majority of attributes we associate with virtual architecture seem to exist far from the world of constructing and building architecture as we know it, the trajectory for the future is one of inevitable convergence of these distinctions. In the future, common architecture will probably merge with what is now developing only as virtual architecture, and it will be one of the next radical breakthroughs in architectural design and discourse.

At Asymptote the computer increasingly plays a vital role in all phases of the design, from sketch to engineering and through to implementation. In this way our work is influenced by digital tools and the new theories emerging today because of them. Virtual architecture, understood here as spatial realms predicated on data and information, undoubtedly influences the ways we now understand space, form, movement, and geometry. Virtual architecture is for the moment manifest mostly within virtual space, and the Internet is a prime protagonist in creating entirely new forms of "dwelling"; but virtual architecture might very well constitute the pioneer effort in forging new forms of real habitation. In other words, the territory in which virtual architecture operates and thrives is a terrific test arena for inevitable futures, and in such an arena we stand to learn a lot about the future of architecture.

Our cities are already under the influence of virtualization, as seen in experiments such as the Virtual LA project, a collaboration by the computer science, physics, and architecture and urban design departments at the University of California at Los Angeles (1998). This project set out to digitize the entire city of Los Angeles in such a way that it allowed people to inhabit a proxy-reality. People were able to view traffic flows, public-transit movement, new building development, and the status of the city's infrastructure. The proposal allowed the citizens of Los Angeles to inhabit both a virtual and a real city simultaneously. For the moment this kind of virtual-reality environment, which other cities like Singapore, Toronto, and Kuala Lumpur are constructing, is based primarily on the existing artifact, which is extrapolated into datascapes for virtual habitation. One can imagine new models and scenarios in which urban plans and strategies begin to incorporate virtual-reality technologies and infuse buildings and infrastructure with digital capabilities that mesh the parallel realities in the future.

Eventually, our need to comprehend and explore cyberspace and virtual reality will prompt us to incorporate these and other tools within architecture, and they will become increasingly compelling. As human beings we are drawn to explore and comprehend the unknown using every capability available to us. Virtual reality holds immense curiosity for us, just as the oceans and the infinite expanse of the universe do.

51

The 19th century witnessed a series of stages in the thrusting progress of a vast aspiration which emerges as the quintessence of the bourgeois ideology of representation. From Daguerre's Diorama to Edison's first Kinetophonograph, each state of the pro-history of the cinema was intended by its initiators — and seen by its publicists — as representatives of their class, as another step taken toward the "re-creation" of reality, toward a "perfect illusion" of the perceptual world.

— Noel Burch, "Charles Baudelaire versus Doctor Frankenstein," *Afterimage* 819 (1981)

As the Internet and other advanced information technologies become exceedingly pervasive promises of fluid interactive environments filled with endless streams of information are imminent. The space of interactivity coupled with the prospects of multimedia are inevitably opening the way for architects to operate within the folds of information space, to develop and devise as yet unforeseen territories for human interaction and dwelling. The World Wide Web, despite its tedious and clumsy structure, already enables one to navigate through vast arrays of information, images, and data. New modeling languages and interfaces are promising improved maneuverability, real–time capabilities, and limitless retrieval and dissemination of information.

Architecture is at a critical juncture. The profession might deny the digital onslaught and claim to be immune to the phenomenology of virtuality, choosing instead to view new technology as only a means to the further entrenchment of architectural representation as "perfect illusion." And yet another claim might be put forward: that architectural representation as we have known it is under siege, and that space and representation are now a single action that the architect is capable of engaging and making evident.

00 KyoZone: Tokyo Extreme
Tokyo is a city that achieves an almost perfect chaos, a place where Eastern traditions and values are offset and thrown into relief by the immediacy and mediation of Western cultural exports.

The KyoZone is an abstraction of contemporary Tokyo formulated as a working prototype of an early twenty-first-century global urbanism that emerges as a montage of events and vivid distortions. The seemingly speculative whims of real estate development, the hallucinatory ethics of consumerism, entertainment, and tourism, and the strange technologies that encapsulate the hypermodern metropolis of Tokyo were all incorpo-rated into the KyoZone. The new architecture was not only the outcome of an already entrenched and strange urbanism, it was effectively an utterance of a new city space that we have yet to inhabit.

01 Smart Space
Every aspect of modern life is being scrutinized against the prospects of "smart technology." Today, acquiring news and information with the aid of smart agents, altering physiological states by means of smart drugs, or designing buildings or objects with smart materials, all point to a future of greater efficiency and certitude. While skyscrapers in Tokyo are being constructed by robots guided by remote computers and America's smart houses are being technologically tailored to a specific ambiance, smartness is increasingly part of the everyday. These technologies are capable of detecting by electronic surveillance metal fatigue in steel structures; they keep tabs on the whereabouts of employees within an office complex; they purportedly differentiate between friend and aggressor for the quick maneuvering of smart bombs. They inevitably impact our built environments.

Architectural advances and visions have never been distinct from technological possibility and change. Historically, our cities and buildings have always been a reaction to (if not a direct result of) technological flux. As an underlying condition of the constant state of change brought to the surface, smart space might emerge with new orders that affect not only our physical environs but also metaphysical states.

To create Smart Space, video images of various digitally derived and animated spaces were projected onto pivoting translucent screens. The existing space was manipulated into several new configurations by means of these projected full–scale speculative environments. Created with light, movement, and surface, this new space of fluctuating meaning posited the architectural possibilities of smart technologies.

02 Kinetic House

The notion of kinetics, as it pertains to space and architecture, has been supplanted by virtual movement. This displacement exemplifies the shift from the machine paradigm to new informational and media structures as major agents of change in our living environments. The contemporary dwelling space, equipped with five hundred-channel TV, interactivity, Internet presence, and home shopping, has immersed us in the paradoxical condition of maximum access and minimum movement.

Transformed by the phenomenal realm of information, the "house" might provide a new space of habitation that reflects the fluctuating conditions that surround and embody it. The Kinetic House addresses the dialectic between the stationary body and simulated movement. It consists of two curvilinear double-skin walls facing away from each other with a passage between them. Digitally manufactured surfaces and environments were projected by video into the cavities of the walls and created an interstitial zone between them as a kind of virtual passageway through the house. The video content presented various "kinetic" structures as assemblies that one could observe, pass through, or dwell in.

03 Media City

The various mechanisms of global deployment and dissemination of information have created auspicious structures, both within and outside the public realm. News on demand, home shopping networks, the Internet, cellular communications, and video conferencing have all created vast arrays of virtual economies and communities. The media itself has attained the status of a self-sustaining culture with efficient and eloquent management of images, concepts, lifestyles, demographics, and politics. Shrouded within these vectors are the new spaces in which we will live, work, and play.

The histories and discourses of twentieth-century visual culture are paramount. Film, painting, performance art, photography, and architecture are implicated in current research as antecedents to contemporary notions of speed, efficiency, control, and delirium.

The cornerstone of Media City was material initially derived from media culture and resampled in the computer to generate new media environments. Here digital technologies are used to unravel certain aspects of media culture and create new architectures for a yet to be understood media-urbanism.

The simultaneous projection of multiple animated digital images onto and through a transparent surface and into an adjacent space beyond created a real-time, large-scale digital space of reverberating mediated phenomena.

04 Alphaworld

This installation consisted of a virtual panopticon that Asymptote called Alphaworld, which is now being constructed on a server in London. Using as a point of departure technologies such as electronic surveillance and global positioning, we generated new spaces that were abstracted through the digital process of their retrieval. The capture of these codified and remote sites impacted the space of observation and recording.

The video content that was used in this installation incorporated movement as a means of formulating enclosure and experience. The type of movement involved challenged the ubiquity of the more generic "fly-through" as a means of navigation and instead proposed panning, retinal scanning, and surveillance as more precise models to be utilized.

The installation was made in a bunker-like space where the main "view" was an interactive forty-foot-long stretch of nine-foot-high video projections. A rear projection on a smaller wall thirty feet away contained mapping information that allowed viewers to comprehend their relative position in the virtual world at any particular moment.

05 E-gora

Agora \Ag"o*ra\, n. [Gr.] An assembly; hence, the place of assembly, especially the marketplace, in an ancient Greek city.

The E-gora is a globally accessible non-place where a virtual public is becoming increasingly present. It consists not only of Internet space and its substrata of e-mail, chat, virtual reality markup language (VRML), and CUseeMe, but also those familiar territories such as public access television, C-SPAN, court TV, and even the voyeuristic spectacles of "caught on tape" programming that are so influential in the vast electro-sphere we now call a community. Other players include the "theme mall," offspring of the Las Vegas Strip, which has further transformed into the simulacra of the new Universal Studios, Disney World, and a slew of other "escapes." These places where the real event is consumed by the virtual spectacle seek cultural legitimacy within the new industry known as Edutainment. The theme restaurant, interactive game, and brand-boutique such as Nike World are all technological mediations on a domestic scale, where hypertextual iconography and flows of information circulate endlessly, making for a marketplace both electronically inflected and imagistically present. As "first reality" manifestations, these locations are effectively the result of the emergence of the E-gora. Where the E-gora continues its transformation toward a global entity within the ether of networks and bandwidth real estate, the local conditions of architecture and urbanism seek a hyperspatiality capable of forming entirely new assemblies and formations.

06 Informing Interiorities: Prototypical Investigations in VRML

The fact that three-dimensional entities can be transmitted and dispensed across the electrosphere is a fundamental extension of Marshall McLuhan's notion that the global village will be formed by virtue of a symptomatic "retribalization." The presence and proliferation of virtual reality markup language (VRML) across the Internet, for example, marks a moment in history when communication technology is meeting the manufacture of space head on. Information and space are now fusing as disembodied circumstances that are mutable, transformational, temporal, and mnemonic.

Architects today have VRML at their disposal as a tool. Its significance, however, lies not in its potential for re-representation of built space as we know it, nor is it the technology that will merely entertain us with virtual worlds. Instead, what might intrigue us as architects is the opportunity to revisit the problematic of perception, the formation of meaning, perspectival certainty, plasticity, and form, coupled with the processes of dislocation, disembodiment, illusion, and distraction.

Experiments with VRML that now dot the Web seem to be conspicuously devoid of architectural content. They are for the most part disembodied presences. How, then, does the architect engage this tool? Can the production of simultaneously "occupied" and transformational space reveal a new spatiality? Do the aspects of record, memory, and mutation afford any spatial possibilities for architecture? Is the transmission of spatiality a form of information-exchange particular to our time?

The Prototypical Investigations in VRML will not only rely on VRML for their manufacture and implementation (and form a theoretical foundation from such action), they will also determine the precise moments of dissonance and rupture between so-called "first reality" space and time.

07 BLUR: An Architecture of Augmented Reality

When speaking of architecture today we are confronted with two distinct realities, one being the physical space of building as we have always known it, predicated on inhabitation and enclosure, and another being the spatiality exported across mediascapes, such as the Web and television. The path that architecture will inevitably follow is one of convergence and blurring. Cities now are navigated, experienced, and comprehended not only as physical locations on maps, or as climate, geography, morphology, and history, but also as "non-places," virtual sites built on touristic propaganda, homepages, advertising campaigns. Architecture will have to contend with these twin realities.

The studio will concern itself with the notion that city space and architecture exist in a mutated condition of the actual. Urban centers, buildings, and spaces might now develop and emerge out of a convoluted feedback loop between actual and virtual reality. One could argue that the outcome is an architecture of accretion, where space and information augment one another, forming a territory of ambiguity and an implicit delirium.

08 Inverse Space: The Museum of Virtual Art

Art museums as we have known them in the past century have reached limits in terms of both meaning and architectural assembly. New demands on the archiving and display of artifacts, images, structures, and writings have prompted a wide range of architectural attempts at housing such production. Frank Gehry's Guggenheim Bilbao has reestablished the museum as both a container for art and a spectacle in and of itself. The question for such an institution is whether the experience of art must compete with the architecture as a commodity. This question also pertains to the contemporary art world itself: Is art a mere reflection, a parallel reality? The crisis is best understood via an entirely new genre of art manufactured by means of digital production, primarily through the Internet. Known as virtual art or cyber art, it seeks legitimacy in the world of fine art. The Internet, a vast wasteland to some and a new frontier to others, is devoid of museum walls and the institutional limits that hinder built museums. Like historic genres (Dada, Abstract Expressionism), cyber art professes to privilege individuality, champion interactivity, assert choice, and encourage protest, thriving on the elimination of borders and controls. Yet the unprecedented immediacy of virtual art propagated through the Web means that a supra-mass consumption is perhaps for the first time a necessary and critical component.

The need for such cultural legitimacy and potency presents itself to the architect as an intriguing problematic in which not only housing and display are considerations but so, too, is every aspect of the institution's public vitality and relevancy — including the gift store.

Virtual art will continue to flourish, some of it created by established artists, some by pretenders, and works will emerge irrespective of the art world's preset expectations and criteria for legitimacy. Criticism, curatorial politics, public opinion, commodification, and the public's insatiable appetite for viewing will also continue. The architect is once again implicated in this future; there will emerge the need for spatialists once again to confront notions of housing, experience, and branding while also providing experience, delirium, possibility, and diversion.

The emergence of a Museum of Virtual Art is inevitably going to take hold in two realms, the virtual and the real. And in both territories it is the architect's expertise that will act as the portal to the works.

The Strategy:
1. Select a media-saturated condition for a city, place, event, or structure.
2. Utilizing the Internet or another electronic medium, formulate a passage or derive.
3. Develop from step 2 a program brief for two simultaneous coexisting architectures, one virtual and one actual.
4. Merge these architectures into an assembly or set of assemblies that could be implemented in a virtual environment and realized as a physical condition. These architectures should revisit the original condition selected in step 1.

Q: What makes your generation different from others?

A: The information/digital age, global economies, biotechnology, information as commodity.

Q: Are these developments significant in relation to various fathers of contemporary architecture, such as Frank Gehry, Peter Eisenman, Rem Koolhaas?

A: The difference is that we are the first generation of architects since the moderns that isn't working beneath the weight of Modernism. The architects you mentioned, as for most of those in their generation, have been steeped in the consciousness of the demigods of Modernism, Mies Van der Rohe, Le Corbusier, Alvar Aalto, etc. Gehry, Koolhaas, Eisenman, and their cohorts have all sought to undo the ties and influences of the avant-garde moderns that preceded them. For us, the heroic modern architects are no longer present, and we are working within a new terrain.

Q: What are the local or cultural influences on your formation as architects (nature, climate, urban morphology, urban sprawl, urban density, city-site, sea-site, colors, lights, construction materials, East Coast/West Coast, etc.)?

A: Noise, distraction, movement, flows, transpacific flight, blur, the Internet, fluxus, plastics, Photoshop, VRML, speed (data), transience, and liquidity.

Q: How early did you start to work with computers?

A: We installed our first machine in 1988 and it ceased to be a paperweight in 1993.

Q: Do you implement software/computers in every phase of your work?

A: Yes, in programmatic approach, conceptual design (diagrams), schematic design (massing), construction drawings, phasing and costs, and presentation layouts.

Q: How does your educational background affect your design?

A: I worked closely throughout graduate school and for a short period afterward with Daniel Libeskind, who at the time was extremely uninterested in computers and almost excessive in his demand for craft and philosophical intentionality. I actually look upon that influence as critical to my own position in relation to the technology we confront today. We don't use computers as mere technological means, but as a multiplicity of tools that aid not only the design process but also the thought process.

Q: Are made-by-hand sketches and models still necessary to produce architecture?

A: Sketches are sometimes still necessary to elucidate ideas and to transfer thoughts quickly to clients and collaborators. Models, on the other hand, are still made in our studio for presentation as studies and records. The analog model, although at times simply a repeat of its digital counterpart, is useful because it remains present after the power is shut down. Therefore, its life is continuous and can be meditated upon. The model is still critical when the project is to be built in first reality. As for our digital environments and architectures, only a few sketches appear and we make no analog models.

Q: How important is the formal aspect in your work?

A: Architects are forever absorbed by the problems of form and formalism. We understand buildings that appear as objects or symbols. But architecture is much more complex than a formal statement or symbolic gesture. We have been interested from the beginning in the field as both source and place into which an intervention is made. From our Steel Cloud project for Los Angeles in 1989 to our Yokohama Bay project in 1996, each work has emerged from the contextual, phenomenal, and cultural strata that surround the site, program, and meaning of the building we were designing. The forms that emerged derive from these strata, as well as from our interpretations and readings. Lately we have become somewhat more interested in generating form through computers. However, we think that computer output is meaningless without the architect's preoccupation with form, and we attempt to reveal other less obvious potentials through its use. When working in virtual reality we discover yet another interesting relation to form: for the most part the architecture is really the result of ephemeral components such as movement, sound, interactivity, luminosity, and narrative.

Q: How is your design conceptual or critical? Is it necessary for your architecture to explore other disciplines, such as natural science, philosophy, literature, the arts?

A: Our work is very much involved in the space between the conceptual and the implementable, and in this way the work is critical and discursive. We are not as interested in bringing the sensibilities of other disciplines to the work as we are compelled to take the work out toward other territories. As we explore the architectural assemblies and ideas we are forming, we tend to merge them with other external interests. For the most part, our peripheral interests include film, mass media, visual arts and culture, and technology.

Q: How do you combine programmatic and functional concerns with conceptual architecture?

A: We do not really differentiate between the programmatic and functional problems of architecture and the so-called conceptual project. Program function, structure, and economy are all equally interesting territories in which to develop a conceptual approach. In this way our work attends to these concerns alongside musicality, flux, distortion, and any other conceptual approach we are engaged in.

Q: Does geometry (Euclidean, fractal, topological, etc.) play a major role in your design?

A: For us geometry in and of itself is not an issue. Each geometric principle or approach offers fascinating and provocative possibilities for architecture. The question is not so much which is the appropriate one to adopt or subscribe to, but rather what does each reveal and imply about the spatiality we are creating. Also, we believe very much in the double life of geometry in architecture, the alliance with structure and economy and the parallel condition of geometry as a mechanism for perception and comprehension.

Q: Do you use diagrams, templates, or partis to generate your architecture?

A: No.

Q: Do you think a computer-generated diagram is a critical instrument that divulges forms?

A: No

Q: Do you use the computer to be transgressive, to resist to normalization?

A: Yes, and for us the computer generates entirely new types of "sketches" in the realm of the filmic, the sonic, the textual, and so on.

Q: Do you produce theoretical writings? How strong is the integration between theory and your practice?

A: A very important component of our work is writing, which, incidentally, is not so much theoretical as it is semiotic play and an attempt to write space.

Q: How do you define your computerized design: Is it fluid, anthropomorphic, organic, striated, folded, topological?

A: Streamed, real-time versus recorded, augmented, interactive, interfaced.

Q: What kind of software do you use in your design process? Is your space design recognizably influenced by it or limited by its capabilities?

A: We use various software without privileging any one in particular. Software today, unlike even a few years ago, is highly malleable. We find that each upgrade and new software that enters the work is even more versatile.

Q: Does the digitized virtual world allow you to generate previously unknown spaces?

A: Producing digital architectures is enabling us to develop worlds and space that are completely new and unprecedented while also allowing us to continue to explore architectural ideas that we have always been interested in but lacked the visionary clients needed to implement.

Q: Is digital work more relevant to conceptual architecture or to built architecture?

A: Simultaneously both.

Q: What is the predominant orientation in your recent work?

A: We are building our second first-reality project at the moment and we are involved in two very ambitious and large-scale virtual architectures for the New York Stock Exchange and the Guggenheim Museum. So the orientation is explicitly asymptotic.

Q: In using technological tools to produce aggregations, does your work risk being more graphic and illustrative than architectural?

A: Perhaps in the short term, and particularly in the schools; but clients, economies, politics, ideology, and culture have a peculiar way of alleviating that problem. And above all, the seamless integration of these tools into our practices and lives will inevitably alter our relation to them.

Christian Pongratz and Maria-Rita Perbellini are architects and writers based in New York. They interviewed Hani Rashid at Asymptote's studio in August 1999.

Q: What were the guidelines and the theoretical principles you followed while working on the Guggenheim Virtual Museum? Does the site have any metaphor of navigation?

A: Both the Guggenheim Virtual Museum (GVM) and the Guggenheim.com projects were thought of as spatial interfaces. However, the two projects' demands and criteria were quite different. Whereas the GVM is primarily thought of as a surrogate or augmented architectural experience that requires geometry, form, space, and time, Guggenheim.com is more informationally loaded, televisory, and encyclopedic. Simply stated, the GVM is thought of as an architectural experience on the Web while Guggenheim.com is a media experience exploring the spatial situation we have become accustomed to through television, film, the book, the billboard, and so on.

Q: What kind of experience should visiting a virtual museum yield?

A: The virtual museum should give the visitor an authentic museum experience, one in which time spent exploring, viewing, and comprehending works of art is meaningful, exciting, and informative. This can be achieved at the GVM for a number of reasons. First, the experience is based on geometric changes in the computer-generated structure, such that one is in control of the architectural assemblies. Second, the work on display is new digital work made especially for the Internet museum experience. And third, the experience is based on time and memory, which is a very real type of experience, the sort of experience we have in real space.

Q: When did you start working on the Guggenheim Virtual Museum and what are the problems that you faced?

A: We began working on the Guggenheim Virtual Museum in 1999, and our biggest problem was making traditional curators understand how exciting and new these virtual spaces could be for artists to work in. The Web is still a frontier and only now are we beginning to understand how to use it effectively. The other hurdle we were up against was technological change: we had ideas and visions for the project that would require more advanced technologies, and indeed the project needs constant updating as new technologies emerge. That's a strange situation but it's the nature of digital and Internet technological progress.

Q: Which other disciplinary practices come close to the way you conceive architecture?

A: We have always found inspiration in filmmaking because it, too, requires that one gain expertise in several areas, combine that expertise with vision and a sense of purpose, and manifest it in such a way that people can access the ideas and vision while experiencing pleasure and gaining knowledge.

Q: How do you and your partner Lise Anne Couture divide the work of Asymptote?

A: We have worked together for many years and have grown and developed simultaneously. We complement each other's creativity and madness with logic and reason. Collaboration and role-switching have been very important to running our practice.

Q: The online universe is expanding. Will it be, in the future, the territory that traditional architects will conquer?

A: Traditional architects will not conquer the Web because they will continue to define architecture as mere building design. Emergent hybrid practices, such as we believe Asymptote to be, are leading the way by marrying ideas about space and form, to experience, electronic interface, and technology. New practices will be as comfortable within the Web as in designing environments. We are quite confident in our abilities to tackle building design, Web design, virtual reality, art installations, furniture design, and any other projects that require innovative explorations of spatial and technological problems.

Q: Tell me about the Guggenheim Virtual Museum and the changes you are making at Guggenheim SoHo (the real time counterpart).

A: The GVM is now substantially complete and being "programmed" with exhibitions. The project began as the Guggenheim's foray into the world of virtual art and the Internet. The premise behind the commission was that there exists now an ever-growing amount of art generated in the electrosphere (the space of the Internet and other digital landscapes and media). That work is not easily collected, housed, and displayed. The GVM is an online museum that contains work generated in the same medium in which the GVM exists. The experience of such work is unique. As far as Asymptote is concerned, the experience is multidimensional, spatial and architectural; that being said, it is obviously necessary that the GVM also be an interface that employs Internet protocols and standards created for the Web. Today the GVM is using Flash, QuickTime, VRML, and other current technologies to enact spatial conditions, but tomorrow it will undoubtedly be reconfigured and perhaps reconstructed entirely using the latest software.

As for the Guggenheim Center for Art and Technology in SoHo, New York, it will be an interesting hybrid space where people will be able to experience the GVM as well as a larger Internet initiative — in real space, in real time. The space is actually thought of as a virtual/real arcade connecting Broadway with Mercer Street through the block. The first reality experience is supplemented and augmented by the access to the virtual environments and the simulation spaces we are planning for the 1,000-square-meter space. The project is the second in a series for which we have been fortunate to create real architecture that is influenced by our virtual commissions. The first was the Advanced Trading Operations Floor for the NYSE after we developed and implemented the 3DTF, a virtual data-environment. In both cases the clients are the ones prompting us to build environments that mesh with the virtual worlds we designed.

Q: What is the difference between a virtual space and a dynamic graphic representation of text and image?

A: Our work with the New York Stock Exchange made this distinction quite explicit for us. NYSE's need to navigate an immense amount of data and information was not being satisfied even by the technical expertise that was at their disposal prior to our involvement with them. It became clear once we were on board that we were being asked to answer the very question you pose and provide a solution they could adopt. We discovered that mere text and image mapping onto three-dimensional environments was not adequate in terms of acquiring knowledge and a deeper understanding of the data. A spatial approach proved to be more effective, and even more successful was an architectural approach. We likened the process to the spatiality we experience when we're driving, flying, or even simply walking through space. Movement implies geometry, and geometry then implicates form, and so on. As we dug deeper into the virtual environment we realized that space, form, time, and information could yield in concert a rich and cognitive spatial experience where memory, experience, reflex, and perception increased the amount of information one could gain from the environment. This is a theory that has been understood for centuries within the notion of memory palaces and religious architectures. In other words, space, when probed in its entirety as encompassing physical and metaphysical conditions, constitutes an architectural environment that is defined identically in both virtual and real locations.

Q: How are the traditional architectural problematics of enclosure, form, and order inflected by the new spatial possibilities and digital technologies? Is the idea of movement you mention something you must apply or is it simply a condition of virtual spaces?

A: Taking the three components (from Sigfried Giedion) you cite — enclosure, form, and order — one sees radical shifts taking place. Enclosure, for example, is no longer tied to the notion of shelter from elements or the delineation of interior environments; the digital posits a problematic of enclosure that is more akin to video — transitional, fluid, fluctuating, territories that accommodate experience rather than program. Our Fluxspace experiments, which we carried out in San Francisco and Venice, were conducted with this notion in mind. Form is under similar scrutiny. Software programs developed primarily for the animation and film industries are now in the hands of many capable young architects. We have access to modeling procedures that will process algorithms to generate all types new architectural artifacts. And order, a vestige of Vitruvian principles still alive in modern and postmodern discourses, seems to be all but completely eradicated at present. The meaninglessness of "order" as we have known it is by no means a complete loss; rather it opens up the possibility to formulate new definitions of what constitutes order, orders based on movement, the temporal, and information flow rather than on typology or proportions.

Q: Why do you think digital art is not being exhibited to its best advantage?

A: Digital art is in its infancy, as is digital architecture. It is extremely interesting and inspiring to be involved in their development. The actual difficulty today in exhibiting digital art is not simply a matter of the usual problem solving or finding some new way to display it, which tended to be the case with two shows dedicated to the subject that were launched in 2001 in the United States. "BitStreams" at the Whitney Museum of American Art in New York and "101010" at the San Francisco Museum of Modern Art (SFMOMA) both made noble attempts to house this fledgling art form in traditional galleries, spaces consisting of walls and rooms under the roof of museum institutions. The failure in both cases stemmed from this awkward and impossible fit. Digital art is being spawned on the Web, in computer systems, perhaps even on WAP devices, cell phones, and so on. And as these art forms emerge the only place it makes sense for them to exist — for the moment, at least — is in their own environments. After all, the salon spaces of the eighteenth and nineteenth centuries evolved into the great museum spaces of the Louvre and the Hermitage, and the SoHo lofts and alternative spaces that gave us modern abstraction are undoubtedly why we have museums like the Tate Modern designed by Herzog & de Meuron or the Guggenheim Museum Las Vegas, designed by Rem Koolhaas. There has always existed an interesting symbiosis between art production, its means and origins, and the space of display, dissemination, or entombment.

Q: Virtual space is a totally different means of construction; it's another realm in which to work. Sometimes, though, virtual spaces are related to real buildings in terms of meaning and space. What do you think about this?

A: Virtual space demands entirely different ways of thinking about "building." After all, its real estate is infinite, and it tends (at least for the moment) to be viewed from singular points of view through an interface. It's constructed within dynamic fluctuating spatiality, there is no gravity governing it, and, above all, it can be shut off. Virtual spaces that mimic real buildings, as in a virtual Barcelona Pavilion or Palace of the Soviets, call to my mind the difference between Norman Rockwell and Mark Rothko. Both are painters, yes, but Rockwell the realist raised the bar on illustration, while Rothko, the abstractionist, perfected canvases that profoundly influence the way we see the world. Obviously, I believe that virtual space has to be about the latter achievement and not a mere reflection of our world as we know it; it's a deep study of possibilities and the unknown.

Q: Why do you think it is necessary to update a virtual building on a continuous basis? It seems that virtual buildings simply have expiration dates. You say that older versions of the Guggenheim Virtual Museums are going to be archived somewhere within the new versions, which sounds like a Russian doll. Can you talk about it? It's difficult to understand the idea of a building that contains itself in another instant of time.

A: It is true that virtual architecture is organic by virtue of its place of origin and occupancy, within the realm of data and information. However, one interesting thing about the organic nature of the Internet is that it is constantly expanding, not unlike our understanding of the universe itself. That being said, the notion of expiration is not really applicable. As the dimensions of data increase, everything remains on record somehow, as a trace or archive. This is why we see virtual architecture as something that needs, like software itself, to be updated in order to sustain the inevitable expansion, while remaining usable and accessible in the face of extreme technological changes. The Russian doll analogy you draw in your question is apropos; the only difference is that in the world of digital technology, each "doll" is in fact an inferior version of the one that engulfs it. In other words, each update and iteration is built on new elevated standards and this allows the virtual entity to evolve over time. This can be witnessed on the Web itself, as we have already seen in its short lifespan and evolution.

Q: What is your process for choosing a language for a virtual building? Your looping, curly forms in the GVM and the aesthetics of the space at the virtual New York Stock Exchange recall a video game, especially in terms of colors and forms.

A: Both these virtual architectures were derived from substantially different needs and programs. The virtual stock exchange embraces a language derived from data mapping and efficient means of acquiring, assimilating, and correlating that data. This drove the aesthetics that you observe as game like. The form and structure were indeed gamelike in so far as video games are nothing more than data-delivery mechanisms through which one has to respond quickly and efficiently. The virtual stock exchange had a similar mandate, an environment meant to convey information quickly and allow one to act on it intuitively, making spatial decisions based on the mandate of the intuition. The Guggenheim Virtual Museum, on the other hand, is a place for the *flâneur*, the wanderer, to borrow a term from Baudelaire. The virtual museum is meant to act as an architectural experience tied to wonder, awe, and memory, a collection of datascapes that one might get lost in or, at the very least, in which one can enjoy a certain kind of delirium.

Q: Museums must generally be neutral boxes that contain art, or else they can be works of art themselves. Virtual museums must be simple interfaces through which to see digital art, or can they be works of digital art?

A: These same dialectics have existed in real museum design for some time — the neutral box versus museum-as-art argument. It is a tired argument in some respects when one looks at the populist success of buildings like Frank Gehry's Guggenheim Bilbao. A more interesting situation for me is how certain museum architectures have affected art and have themselves been influenced by art. Frank Lloyd Wright's Guggenheim Museum is a building that fascinates on a number of levels in terms of this argument. It was designed in an era of mass industrialization and machine-age obsessions, and art was developing under the same circumstances. Cubism, Futurism, and Purism all exerted an impact on Wright and their influence emerged in the powerful spirals of his design. Then Wright's building did something completely unexpected: it influenced artists. Painters and sculptors no longer saw their work relegated to closed salons for viewing. The fact that works could be viewed in the Guggenheim from over thirty meters away must have had profound resonance in the world of contemporary art. Jackson Pollock, Ad Reinhart, James Rosenquist, and Robert Rauschenberg, just to name a few, were in some respects artists who developed and emerged because of the very emergence of buildings like Wright's. The argument of architecture-as-art versus architecture-for-art was exhausted quite eloquently with the emergence of that building in the mid-twentieth century.

Q: How do the GVM and the entire virtual realm complement the physical environment of today?

A: The GVM does not complement the physical environment. Instead it is a place for new artists who might not even exist yet to formulate new works, new ways of envisioning the world, and new avenues of thought. It is a place for virtual art, not the analog art we already know so well. The GVM is a beta museum for art that we don't even yet know exists.

Federico Chiara is a writer and critic based in Milan. This online interview with Hani Rashid for *Italian Vogue* took place in August 2001.

Q: How did Asymptote come about and where are you based?

A: We originally started in Milan, Italy, and then moved the studio to New York in 1989. Asymptote started as an interdisciplinary architectural practice founded by myself and Lise Anne Couture, incorporating a strong interest in experimentation and dealing primarily with spatial theory. In 1995, partially because I co-initiated the Digital Design Studios at Columbia University's Graduate School of Architecture, we became very interested in digital media and its influence on architecture and spatiality.

Q: What does the name Asymptote mean?

A: It is a mathematical term defining the infinite progression of a hyperbolic curve as it approaches an axis; in other words, an infinite meeting point of two converging lines, the vanishing point. This was an appropriate term for us because it symbolized the virtual meeting point of theory and practice, two things we are interested in bringing closer and closer together without actually contaminating one another, two autonomous trajectories. In 1995 Asymptote acquired another meaning for us, that of the pursuit of both virtual and real architecture — again, two parallel tracks that meet at the infinite.

Q: What is Asymptote's design and creative philosophy?

A: Our design philosophy is really based on the idea that spatial experimentation today takes hold in many diverse areas and therefore requires extreme lucidity, versatility, and innovation on the part of designers and architects. We approach each project, whether it is in first reality or in virtual reality, as holding the potential for new experiences, forms, and meaning. In this way we are somewhat detached from pursuing mere formalistic, stylistic, and commercial viability. Instead, we strive to create hybrid entities that implicate these interests while still remaining experimental and provocative.

Q: What about your work ethic, the Asymptote creative process?

A: Our creative process usually involves a great deal of time with trial runs and experiments. We have used the setting of the art gallery as a place to explore ideas under circumstances that tend to be more liberating than client-based work. Our work at the 2000 Venice Biennale and our projects for the São Paulo Bienal and Documenta XI in Kassel, Germany, are all installations that employ digital technologies to alter and augment space. They allow us to explore and understand new ways of designing and developing architectures and "spatial interface."

Q: Where do you draw your inspiration from?

A: Artists and technologists who deal primarily with spatial ideas and conceptual explorations inspire us. The list is very broad and includes the work of the MIT Media Lab, experimental films by people like Stan Brakhage, music by people like conceptual guitarist Glen Branca and composer John Cage, minimalist composer Terry Riley, performances by choreographers William Forsythe and the Frankfurt Ballet, Dada, surrealist Marcel Duchamp. . . . We are also inspired by advances in industrial design, software development, new technologies; also, to some extent, we even look to the special-effects and automotive manufacturing industries. Our work is varied and so are our interests.

Q: What are your current projects?

A: We just completed a new line of system furniture for Knoll International. We are building a pavilion in Holland near Schipol Airport that will be entirely covered in a thin moving surface of cascading water. We are also involved in ongoing work with the New York Stock Exchange, developing a three-dimensional user interface for trading and analyzing stocks and markets on the Internet, as well as a blue-screen simulation environment for

63

broacast television. We are competing for a new building commission for Mercedes Benz in Stuttgart as well as a theater in Copenhagen. We completed the Guggenheim Virtual Museum, located on the Internet, and the design for the new Guggenheim SoHo in Manhattan.

Q: What determines which projects you will pursue?

A: An inspired client, an intriguing brief, an amazing place, or a powerful new technology or challenge.

Q: Tell us a little bit about the Lego LZone in Denmark. How did this project begin? Did you experience any epiphanies while engaged in it?

A: In 1996 we constructed a large-scale work in Aarhus, Denmark, entitled the Univers Theater. This structure covers 30,000 square feet of space at the historic center of the town and is erected each year for their international theater festival. Having been somewhat successful with that we were approached by our client and Lego to develop a project that would help the toymaker change its image to meet the expectations of children and young adults who have become more comfortable and savvy with new technologies like the Internet. This coincided with Lego's own initiatives in the toy market to create "mindstorms" and other technologically "smart" toys that were developed with the MIT Media Lab, where Lego researched and produced its new robotic and electronic toy lines. We designed a physical environment for the Lego company that would allow people to get a sense of the lab setting, interact with each other, and share their own innovative ideas. The architecture derived from the mathematical aspects of algorithmic play, and we became inspired by what we called the invisible Lego block, which is the curvilinear space that contains the attachable side of a Lego block and is made up of circular parts that interlock. We essentially extracted the negative space and created large-scale environments that evoked that space, and then infused the entire environment with information feeds, fiber networks, and flat-panel displays. The building materials could change color according to data inputs.

Q: What would the Asymptote blueprint of Utopia look like?

A: Technology is here to stay and will undoubtedly continue to evolve, so we have a couple of paths to take: either we continue to allow it to dominate our lives, work environments, and cities without paying much attention to it as architects and designers, or we develop strategies and methods that involve technology in terms of our human needs and desires. What we are most focused on is building inspired worlds, be they domestic, institutional, urban, or digital. To do that we need to embrace things like culture, art, and theory along with technology.

Q: What would the Asymptote playground look like?

A: Urban, loaded with smart technologies and surfaces, no straight lines whatsoever, infused with soundscapes to complement the real sounds, and totally reconfigurable.

Q: Where do you think virtual architecture is heading in terms of spatial experimentation?

A: We will continue to see experiments with the virtual that leave the confines of the screen, and that merge the virtual with the real, spaces that will ultimately blur the distinctions of what we currently think constitutes a real experience versus a virtual experience.

Q: What is the most gratifying thing about your profession?

A: That it (architecture) is in a state of complete disrepair and open for total reconfiguration.

Q: If you weren't one half of Asymptote, what would you be?

A: Half a being — or else a filmmaker.

Q: How important is architecture for the urban modernist?

A: Old architecture is as important as it has always been, to dignify city space and function well. New architecture, on the other hand, is important for different reasons; it must be a seamless part of contemporary existence in cities, part of the fluid reality that is cityspace, responding to movement and information. New urbanism has to embrace the digital era, be dynamic, and create a sense of awe that surpasses that of familiar images and electronic interfaces.

Q: What is your take on form and function?

A: Form augments function and function mutates form.

Putri Trisulo is an editor for *Transmission*, a Webzine produced in Singapore. This online interview with Hani Rashid took place in August 2001.

For Asymptote, architectural installations in gallery settings have always served to inform and reveal the theoretical intentions behind a body of work, which has included building designs, city planning, object design, and virtual-reality environments. Our early installations tended to be thought of as one-to-one built environments, where various narratives or programs could take hold. These installations, such as the Kursaal for An Evacuee (1987) held at Artists Space in New York, and the Optigraph Installation (1992) at the Aedes Gallery in Berlin and L'Arsenale in Paris, were based on our feeling that the gallery experience is best understood as a transformational one that can yield new architectural formations and propositions. The privilege of the gallery intervention is that it takes place within a space controlled and delineated by its separation from and simultaneous inhabitation of the real city space. In these sorts of spaces, Asymptote effectively suspends reality to perform a reinterpretation of the world as autonomous and introspective — a world in which architecture transports the inhabitant to places where paper proposals simply cannot. Installations such as our Ocular New York interventions exhibited at the Aedes Gallery in Berlin (1994) created spaces and architectures that encompassed and contained the experience of a new spatiality inspired and instigated by optic experiments and filmic logic. The space of the exhibition hall was transformed into a machine for viewing and comprehending, a sort of suspended reality.

In June 2000 the United States Pavilion at the Venice Biennale was transformed through a collaboration between Asymptote and Hani Rashid's students at the Columbia University Graduate School of Architecture. Through a process of computer digitization, a gymnast was recorded moving through the interior space of the pavilion. Information concerning the body's movement was transferred to a computer using modeling procedures and reconstructed with the assistance of CNC manufacturing technologies. The resul was a built, full-scale architectural intervention based on the mathematics of a body's movement through the actual space of the exhibition pavilion.

Another work built in Venice for the Biennale was a large structure by Asymptote titled Fluxspace 2.0. This outdoor installation measured thirty meters in length and rose two stories in height. The form and structure, a combination of steel frame and pneumatic envelope, created a tangible oscillation between the physical exterior and the fluid, continuously reconfigured state of its interior. The work housed two 360-degree Web cameras set within two circular rotating mirrors located in the Fluxspace interior. As a visitor approached the structure and entered it beneath the pneumatic shell, he or she experienced an interior world under transformation. The rotating one-way mirrors were constantly in motion, and through their quasi-transparency one could see the interior space in a constant state of change and reassembly. The visitor was forced into an ambiguous relationship with the architecture, somewhere between its real condition and its augmented state. This experience of interior flux was enhanced by the Internet images that were broadcast at thirty-second intervals throughout the five-month duration of the exhibition. The camera captured and catalogued some 1.6 million variations on the space's interior.

A related installation carried out by Asymptote in 1999 as part of the California College of Arts and Crafts (CCAC) artist-in-residence program in San Francisco was titled Fluxspace 1.0. This was an attempt at creating a full-scale interactive architectural work and was predicated on the notion that as an installation it could act as a conduit between physical experience and virtual manipulation, particularity with respect to spatial entities. As one approached the work and touched its surface, the "architecture" responded and changed its physical and morphological condition in real time. This change was realized by tethering the large construction to computer systems that responded by way of proximity sensors embedded into the structure's surface. The notion that the installation was a place to house an artificially intelligent architectural entity allowed Asymptote to use the gallery as a sort of conceptual and spatially privileged "wind tunnel." This was effectively an enactment of an architectural experiment prior to its full-scale implementation as a building or another element of urban space.

Virtual architectural environments as augmentations of physical space offer the opportunity to create unique spatial experiences and challenge our definition and understanding of what constitutes movement within "real" environments and "actual" spaces. The evolution of these fluid architectures will be interesting to follow as architects become less concerned with differentiating between the physical and the virtual, becoming instead preoccupied with redefining what actually constitutes a new spatiality and how we in fact move within it. Ultimately, it is within the installation space where these sorts of theses and assumptions can best be tested. For Asymptote, the exhibition space is a place for experimentation, and this is crucial to the research and vision of futures and possibilities in architecture.

Installing Space was first published in *The Art of Architecture Exhibitions*, published by NAi Publishers, 2001.

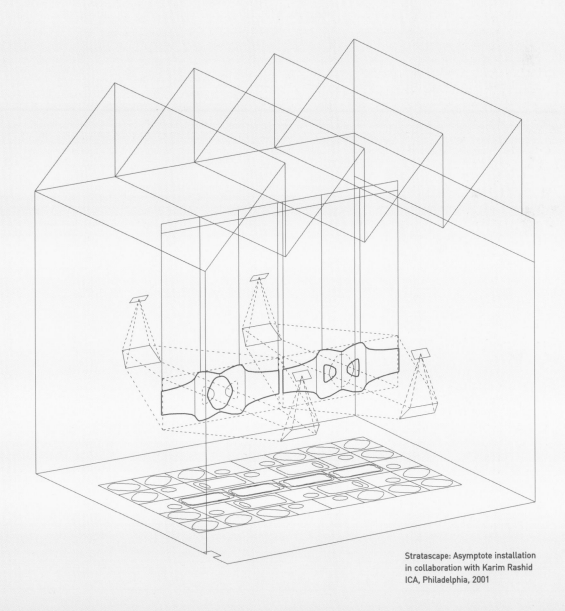

**Stratascape: Asymptote installation
in collaboration with Karim Rashid
ICA, Philadelphia, 2001**

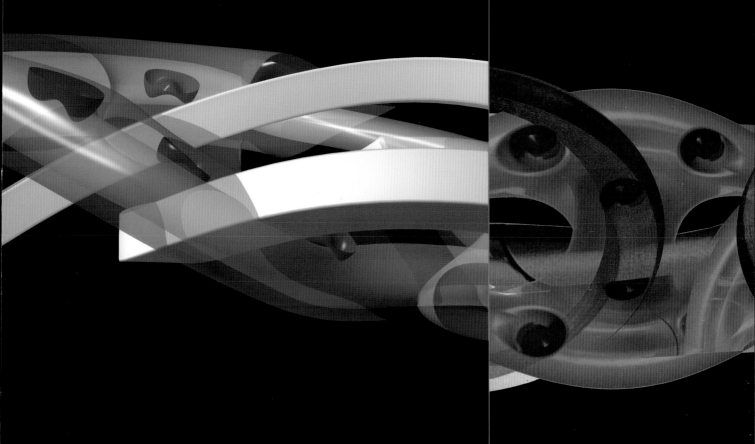

When speaking of an architecture for the next millennium one must consider two conditions: that the physical space of architecture as we have always known it (enclosure, form, and permanence) will without a doubt persevere; and that it will exist alongside the virtual architecture, surfacing in the digital domain of the Internet. Buildings, institutions, spaces, and objects are now being constructed, navigated, experienced, comprehended, and altered in their virtual states by countless people across global networks. This new architecture of liquidity, flux, and mutability is predicated on technological advances and fueled by a basic human desire to probe the unknown. The path that both architectures, the real

and the virtual, inevitably take will be one of convergence. Historically, architecture has struggled with this dialectic of the real and the virtual: Architecture's stability and actuality have always been tempered by the metaphysical and the poetic.

The Guggenheim's own history, architectural vangardism, and cultural significance will form a unique scaffolding for the museum of the future. By combining the richness of this tradition with the potential offered by state-of-the-art digital technnologies, Asymptote aims to create a new architectural paradigm. The Guggenheim Virtual Museum will not only provide global access to all Guggenheim museums, including typical

museum services, amenities, archives, and collections, but also provide a unique and compelling spatial environment to be experienced by the virtual visitor. In addition, the virtual museum is an ideal space for deploying and experiencing art and events created specifically for the interactive digital medium. Here, simultaneous viewing and participation are possible by an audience around the globe. As envisioned by Asymptote, the Guggenheim Virtual Museum will emerge from the fusion of information space, art, commerce, and architecture to become one of the most important virtual buildings of the twenty-first century.

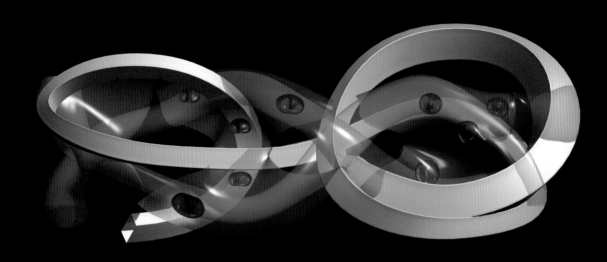

> **GALLERIES** / VIRTUAL ARCHITECTURE GALLERIES

0.0° —

80.0° —

180.0° —

270.0° —

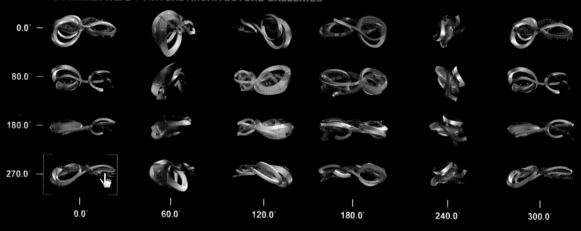

0.0°   60.0°   120.0°   180.0°   240.0°   300.0°

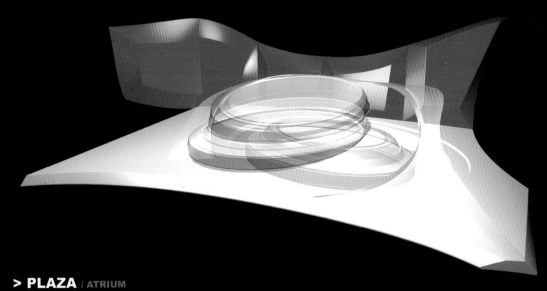

> **PLAZA** / ATRIUM

80.0° —

180.0° —

270.0° —

0.0°   60.0°   120.0°   180.0°   240.0°   300.0°

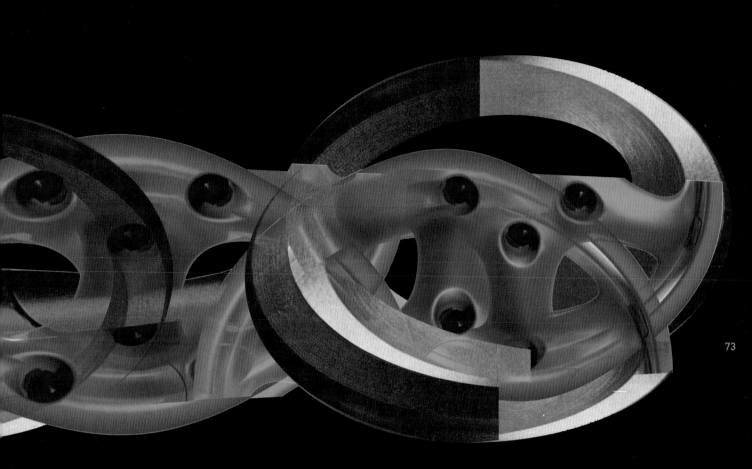

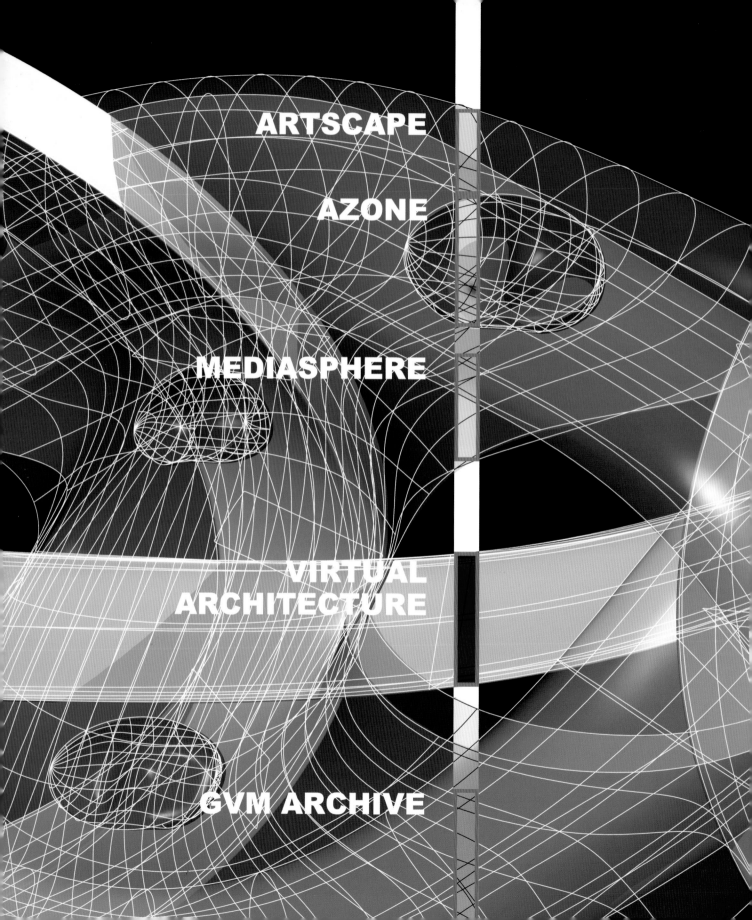

ARTSCAPE

AZONE

MEDIASPHERE

VIRTUAL
ARCHITECTURE

GVM ARCHIVE

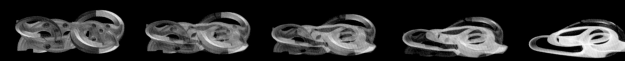

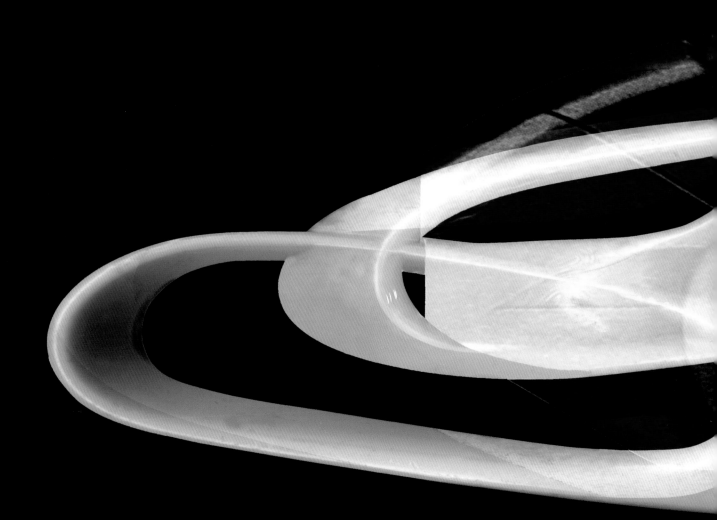

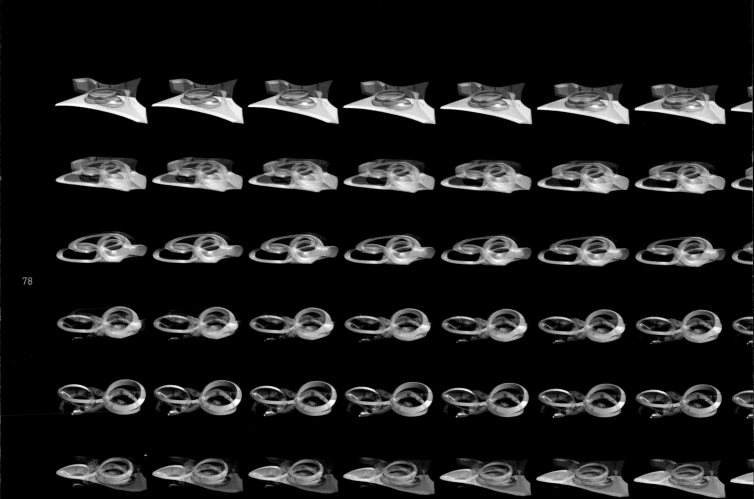

78

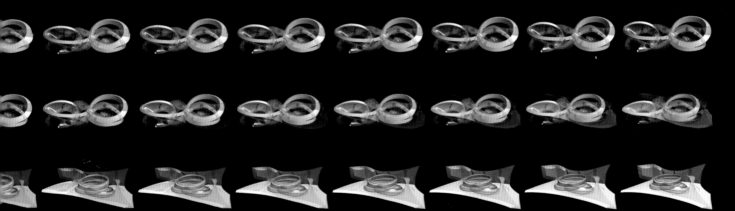

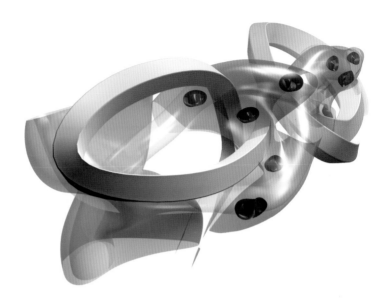

GUGGENHEIM VIRTUAL MUSEUM STUDIES

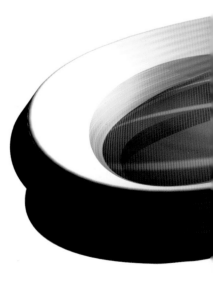

BMW Event and Delivery Center
Munich, Germany

The proposed BMW Event and Delivery Center architecturally embodies the sophistication and advanced technology associated with BMW. The building itself is seen as an extension of the corporate identity and progressive design of the products inside. The interior is a fluid space that creates a dynamic theatrical event out of the design, production, and purchasing of BMW products.

The building consists of two interlocking components: the BMW Event Center and the BMW Delivery Center. The two spaces are physically divided but visually connected. The two primary circulation types are pedestrian and automotive. These two systems overlap and wrap each other, facilitating views from the Event space to the Delivery space and vice versa. Circulation throughout the building is enclosed primarily by glass, so spaces that are physically separated can be viewed through a fluid and transparent architecture.

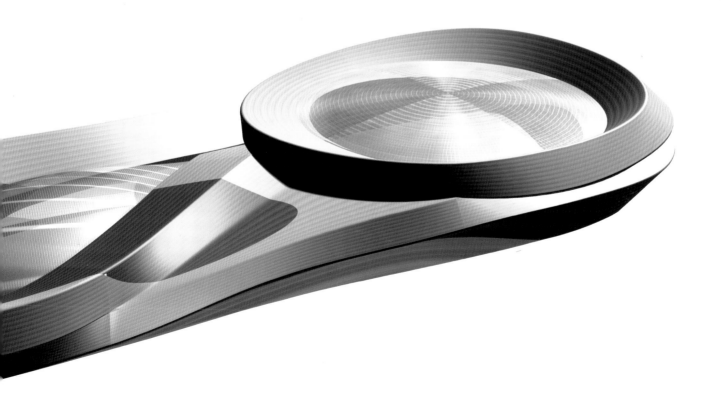

Visitors throughout the building can view
the arrival, delivery, and purchase of BMW
products. Glass-enclosed circulation ramps
wrap around the space, defining the form
of the building and creating a fluid, constantly
changing interior of people and products.
The automobile itself is the focus of the
interior program, thus becoming an integral
part of the experience of the entire building.

82

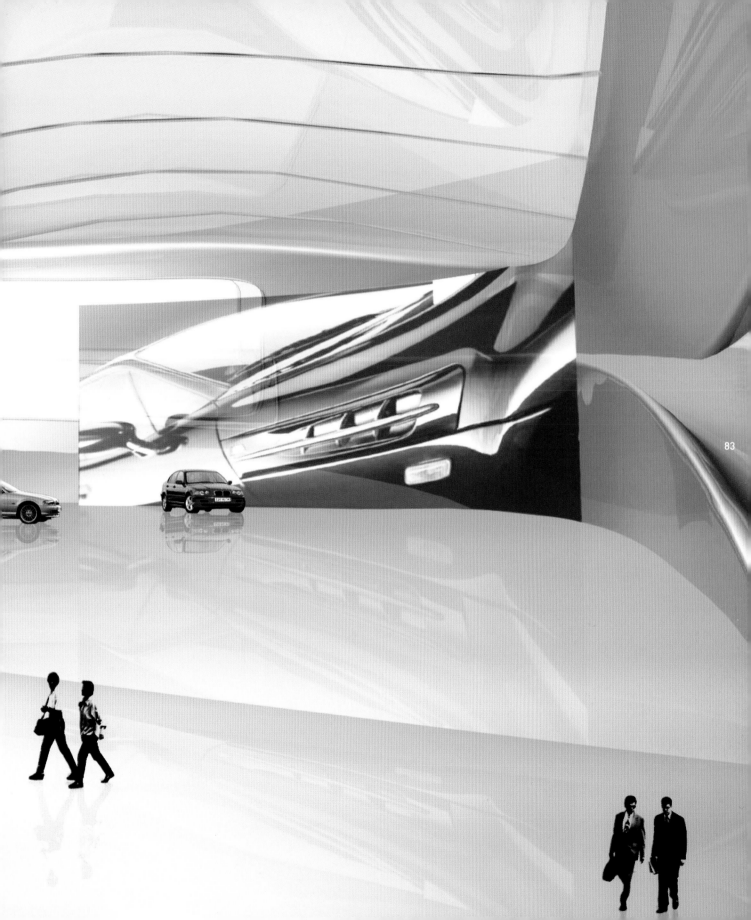

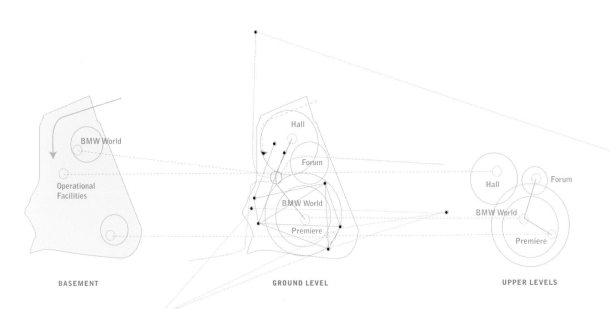

BASEMENT

BMW World

Operational
Facilities

GROUND LEVEL

Hall

Forum

BMW World

Premiere

UPPER LEVELS

Hall

Forum

BMW World

Premiere

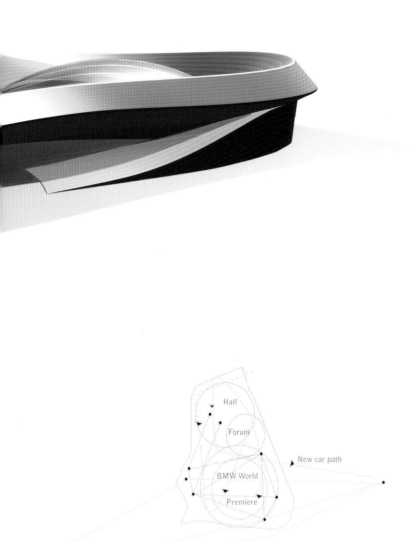

The architecture is intended to be open to its surroundings: a platform from which to view various exhibitions, or a backdrop for car shows. From the upper level there are exterior views to BMW headquarters and to the adjacent 1972 Olympic Park. The path that winds around the building opens up to become an exterior terrace overlooking an outdoor exhibition area in the park. A public path in the form of a ramp connects the BMW headquarters to the Olympic Park. An exhibition of the history of BMW runs along this path. This self enclosed ramp moves through the building without spatially connecting to it but still allows views to the interior.

The entry at ground level is a large, naturally lit glass enclosure. At the entry level are three main public functions that are visually connected: BMW World, an exhibition space; Forum Function Hall, a lecture and perform-ance space; and the shops that surround both areas in the hall.

Above this, Level 1 contains commercial functions and ramps up to the Premiere Delivery Area, where BMW purchases are made and products brought to the customer during a ceremonial event viewable from the Event Center.

RAMP LEVELS

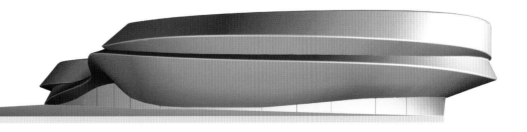

The upper level contains lounges, exhibition spaces, and a roof garden with a view to the Olympic Park. From this upper level the customer drives his or her new BMW down an undulating path that weaves through the building. In this way a purchase becomes an event that activates the interior space of the building.

The Event and Delivery Center uses new material technologies developed in both architectural and automotive design, including compound, curved metal elements in the facade. Sophisticated fresnel lenses are used in the glass over the exhibition space. These rotating glass screens direct sunlight into the atrium and allow the quality of light to be adjusted. Throughout the building, new-media technology is integrated into the architecture, enabling every area to be used as an exhibition/ performance space and further immersing the visitor in the BMW experience.

86

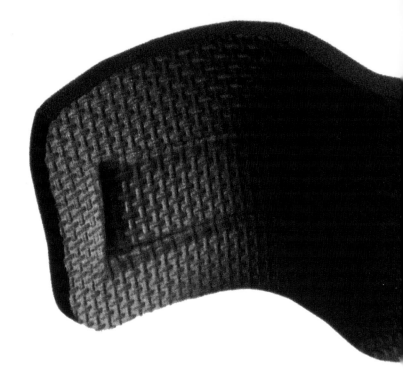

WIPO: BUILDING FOR THE
TWENTY-FIRST CENTURY
Asymptote's entry for the invited competition to design an addition to the
headquarters of the World Intellectual
Property Organization, a specialized
agency of the United Nations, is a scheme
that reflects the institution's mission to
promote communication and cooperation
worldwide as well as to project the importance of technological advancements with
respect to WIPO's increasingly significant
role globally.

LANDSCAPE
The site planning and massing scheme
integrate the new building with the existing
building to form a cohesive complex with a
new centralized entrance and drop-off that
serve the entire site.

Through the manipulation of the ground
plane, a new landscape rises up and over
the new grade-level link between proposed
and existing buildings. This provides a fluid
yet eventful pedestrian connection from
route de Ferney to the area along chemin
des Colombettes as well as a direct connection to the exterior court space of the
new building. This open outdoor court can
be used for special events or enjoyed by
the WIPO staff. It is accessible both from
within the new building and from other
parts of the site.

World Intellectual Property
Organization Headquarters
Geneva, Switzerland

BUILDING

The architecture of the new building complements the existing structure through its form and materials.

The transparent building envelope celebrates views, the natural landscape, and openness. From the use of glass throughout to the deployment of visualization technology within, to the large glass-covered oculus in the new court space open to the foyer below, the architecture conveys a commitment to openess and transparency that is critical to WIPO's mission.

While the facade's materiality supports the philosophical underpinnings of the project, it also contributes to the architecture's technological and environmental sophistication. The double-skin system of enclosure allows users to control natural ventilation and sunlight, and promotes energy efficiency. The metallic mesh of the exterior acts as both a sun-shading device and a sleek facade, in keeping with the architecture of the existing building. A running track on the roof, which is accessible from the health club on the upper floor of the building, offers a unique vantage point and creates an interesting elevation viewed from the adjacent existing WIPO building.

SPACE

The scheme includes a new space at ground level that is a common point of entry for both buildings. This space includes a new reception area and a new public exhibition space with video displays that render the connection between the two buildings eventful and dramatic.

This entrance area also fluidly links the public space of the new building with that of the existing one and allows a direct connection between the conference areas, meeting rooms, and other amenities in both locations.

Public amenities, including the conference halls, can be accessed directly from the public lobby and foyer of the new building. The lobby is infused with digital advanced-visualization technology for the display of live events and the communication of WIPO goals and accomplishments.

The office floors are single-loaded with an open plan, allowing for maximim flexibility in the work areas and views out to the city. Staff amenities and meeting rooms project into the court space to create the architecture of the interior court curtain wall. This vertical "terrain" of glass surrounding the new court area meanders and undulates to form an external crystalline space. The exterior court itself is directly accessible from the public spaces, including the dining areas and library.

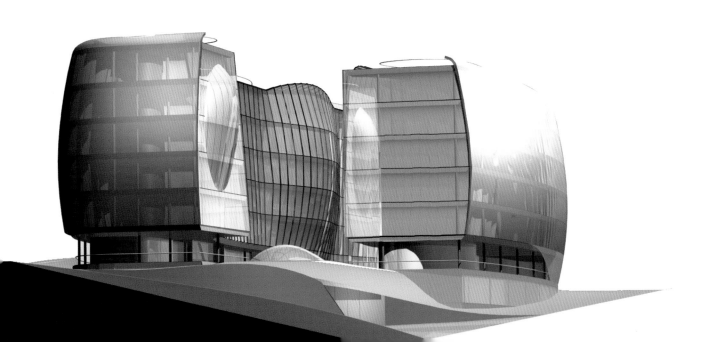

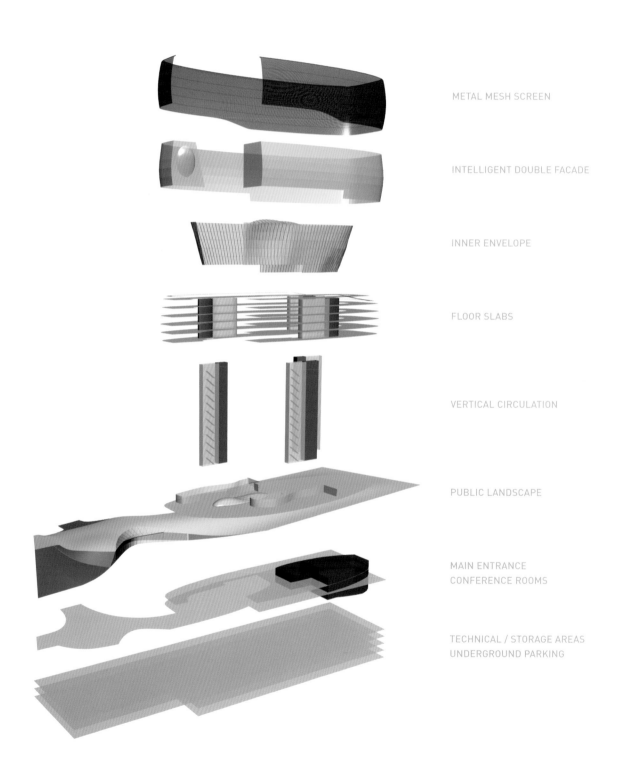

METAL MESH SCREEN

INTELLIGENT DOUBLE FACADE

INNER ENVELOPE

FLOOR SLABS

VERTICAL CIRCULATION

PUBLIC LANDSCAPE

MAIN ENTRANCE
CONFERENCE ROOMS

TECHNICAL / STORAGE AREAS
UNDERGROUND PARKING

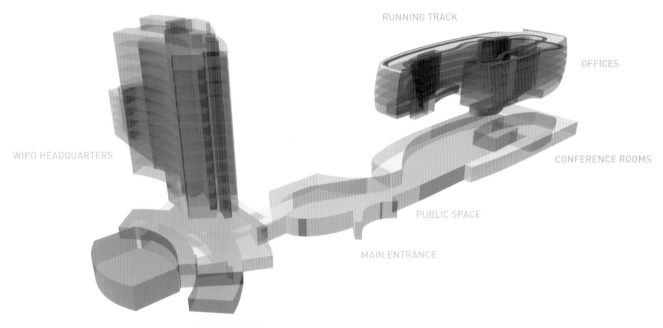

RUNNING TRACK

OFFICES

WIPO HEADQUARTERS

CONFERENCE ROOMS

93

PUBLIC SPACE

MAIN ENTRANCE

CONFERENCE ROOMS

Univers Theaters
Aarhus, Denmark

The Univers Theater, a temporary structure first erected in Aarhus, Denmark, in 1997, brought architecture, theater, and media technologies to the intersection of event-structure and historic presence.

94

95

The aim of the project was to provide an architecture in keeping with the goals of the prestigious Aarhus International Theater Festival, one that would anticipate and incorporate multimedia technologies and prompt social exchanges (virtual and actual) in the historic Bispetorv Square at the center of Aarhus. In addition to implementing structural and mediated technologies, Asymptote created an architecture of hybrid form, unorthodox materiality, and efficient structure to address the critical position of a new architecture confronting the contemporary urbanism of European cities today.

The Univers project was prompted and inspired by both practical considerations and the inherent possibilities of creating a new spatiality within the city center. The temporary structure needed to be not only cost effective and easily assembled but also flexible and adaptable, in anticipation of numerous changes over the next decade. The architecture of the Univers is fully reconfigured from year to year to accommodate and reflect the annual festival theme.

The unique tensile structural system proved ideal for developing a specific image for the festival itself, and for generating future possibilities for the coexistence of the traditional and the new. The structural system, similar to sail-and-mast technology, creates a field condition of illuminated surfaces and objects in the main city square. The disparate and strangely cropped views of the theater frame the surrounding buildings and draw attention to their elegance and architectural value. The structure responds to multidirectional approaches and to the configuration of the square itself. Its non-orthogonal geometry creates animated yet continuous spaces that contain a diverse range of functions.

As the project developed further it also became apparent that the use of tensile materials afforded other possibilities, namely that of a play between an illuminated light structure and the phenomenon of light itself animating the interior and exterior surfaces. The use of light through video projection fuses digital technologies with the semi-transparent material of the architecture. This translucency engages the surrounding context with the interior of the theater and the events occurring within it. The structure captures light and transmits it to its exterior and its surrounding context, thus increasing its scale and impact. Illumination also greatly enhances the space of the surrounding square by making the facades of the adjacent buildings part of the space of the new structure, emphasizing in particular the grandeur of the cathedral and the classical theater that flank the square.

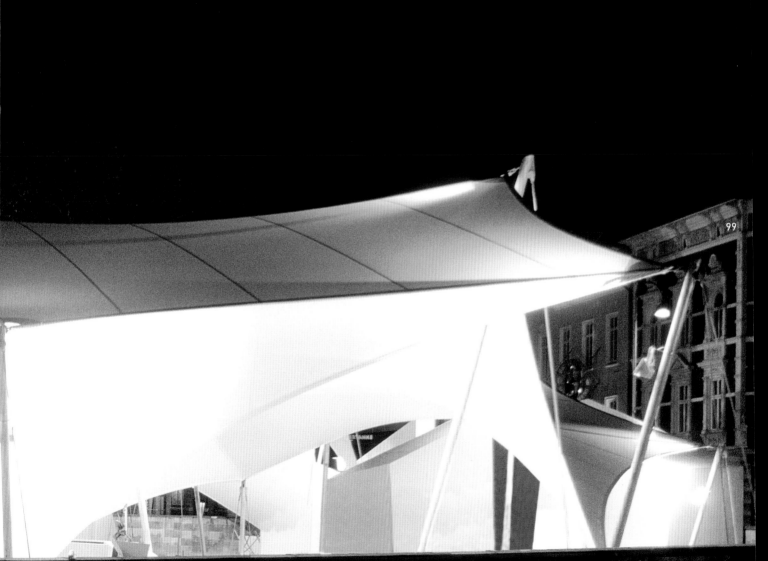

The actual range of digital technologies implemented in the project will become quite extensive over time. The initial video projections served as links to remote sites in the form of digital transmissions of performances simultaneously broadcast locally and globally. There were live television broadcasts as well as public Internet access through individual computer terminals. The Univers was divided into three categories: Social Space, in the form of a restaurant, a cafe, and a bar; Information Space, which consisted of projection and television technology as well as the public computers; and Performance Space, which included up to three stages fully equipped with video screens and sound systems accommodating a wide range of theater, music, and multimedia events. The architecture encourages simultaneous events while maintaining openness and transparency to provide multiple experiences relevant to the the festival, the city, and its culture.

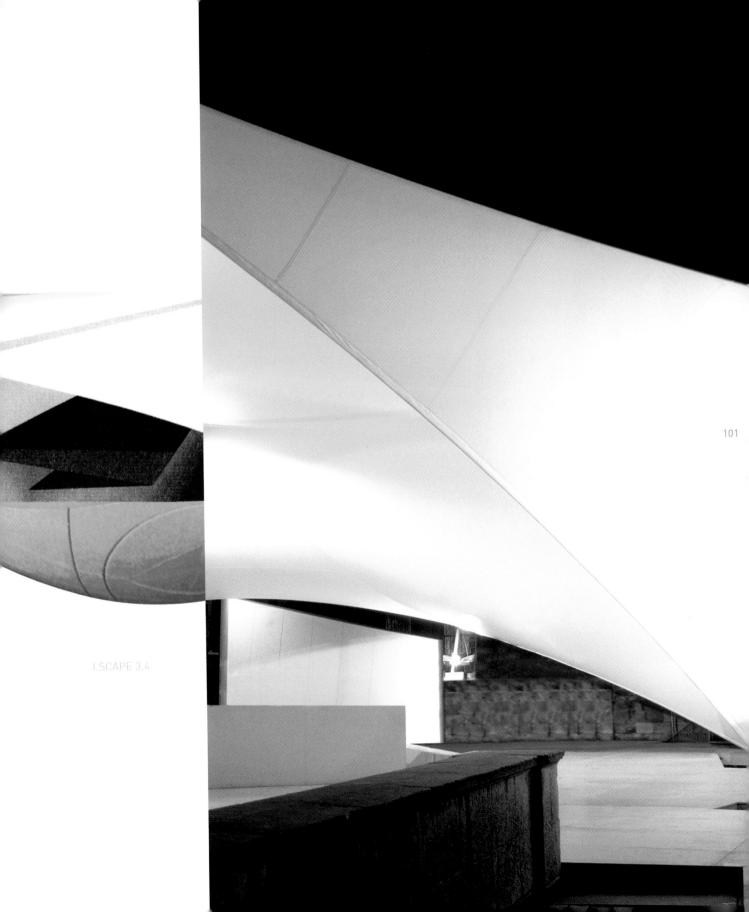

I.SCAPE 3.4

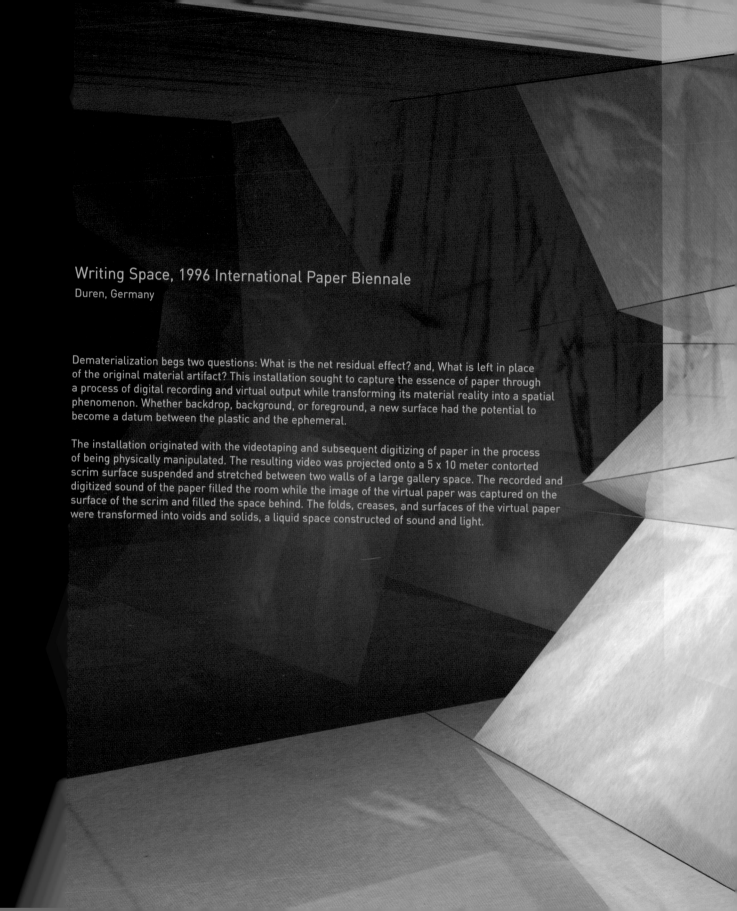

Writing Space, 1996 International Paper Biennale
Duren, Germany

Dematerialization begs two questions: What is the net residual effect? and, What is left in place of the original material artifact? This installation sought to capture the essence of paper through a process of digital recording and virtual output while transforming its material reality into a spatial phenomenon. Whether backdrop, background, or foreground, a new surface had the potential to become a datum between the plastic and the ephemeral.

The installation originated with the videotaping and subsequent digitizing of paper in the process of being physically manipulated. The resulting video was projected onto a 5 x 10 meter contorted scrim surface suspended and stretched between two walls of a large gallery space. The recorded and digitized sound of the paper filled the room while the image of the virtual paper was captured on the surface of the scrim and filled the space behind. The folds, creases, and surfaces of the virtual paper were transformed into voids and solids, a liquid space constructed of sound and light.

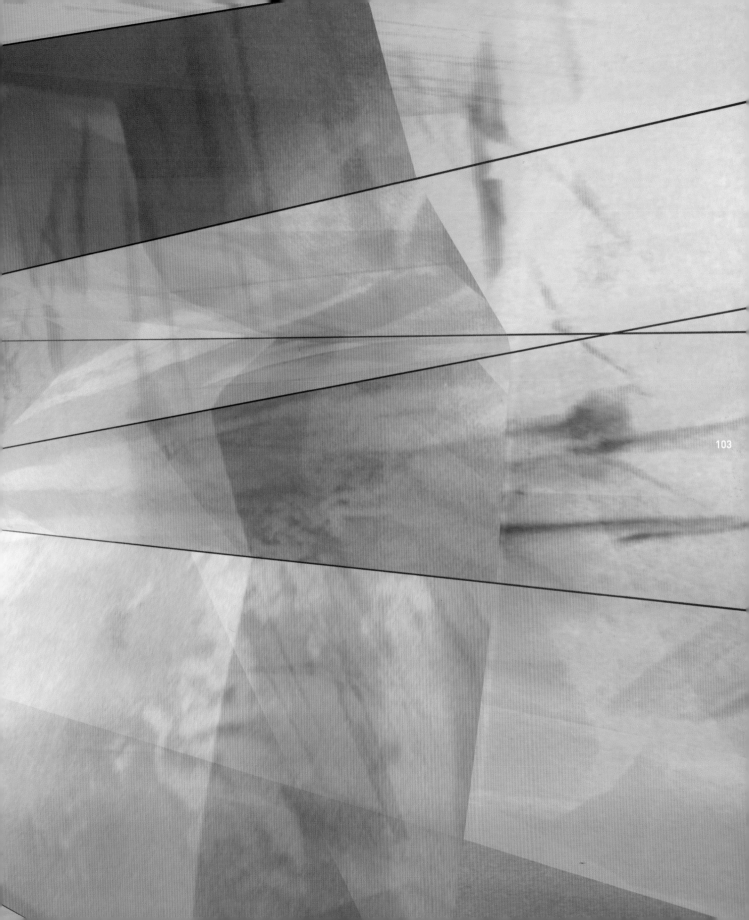

PROCEDURES:

INTERROGATION: of the absence of materiality
MANIPULATION: capturing and transforming the essence of paper
COMBINATION: paper + light, paper + sound, paper + movement
ELIMINATION: of paper as object
EXPLORATION: of the enigmatic domain of representation
DIGITAL TRANFORMATION: translation into phenomena
DEMATERIALIZATION: the manufacturing of a virtual paper
CONSTRUCTION: of the spatiality of making
FORMATION: of surfaces through the tattooing of space
INHABITATION: of the texture map — Writing Space

107

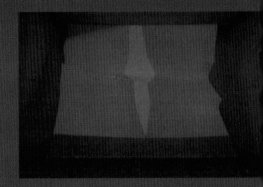

PAPER TRAILS: TZARA'S MEANDER
Cutting, shredding, crimping, folding, wetting a sheet of paper is always a beginning, emptiness is a surface on which we act. A crumpled piece of paper as a start. The discarded paper, a gesture, a scrawl. Writing is a form of drawing and drawing is a way to fill out the paper's potentiality, a single line traversing a sheet of pristine white paper begins an exquisite ending.

Origami, scrolls, newsprint, pulp, pulp-fiction, literature, treatises, codices, paper mill, paper pulp, bleached paper, reams, pounds, tones of paper, the end of paper, paper shredder, paperless office. Binding, crimping, waxing, sealing, filing, and burning paper. Auto da fe, paper rolls, paper weights, tissue paper, and paper plates. A paper trail one leaves behind, newspapers on every surface, and a wall papered with anaglyphs. Paper planes, liquid paper, paper samples, textured papers. Tracing paper, fax paper, clean sheets of paper, mounted, glossy, and semi-matte. Paper boats always float, cutting out, gluing on, strips, shreds, headlines, all that is fit to print. The press, the standard, a paperboy delivers, carrying your papers, a folder filled with documents, tickets, checks, receipts, envelopes, paper dolls. Paper masks, stationery, duplicates, enlargements, a machine that collates, sorts, reduces, and enlarges. Billboards, cardboard, wrapping paper, paper thin, stamped, embossed, and sealed. Historical papers, certificates, marriage licenses, a house of cards, and papers upon which we tread. Coupons, wrapped, masked, and taped. Lost papers, sacred scrolls, signed, absorbent, watermarked. Pliable, subtle, crisp, toothed, cold-pressed, hot-pressed. Paper racks, three-ring binders for lined paper, graph paper, note paper, invoices, paper money, sign the . . . . paper, thin and out of paper.

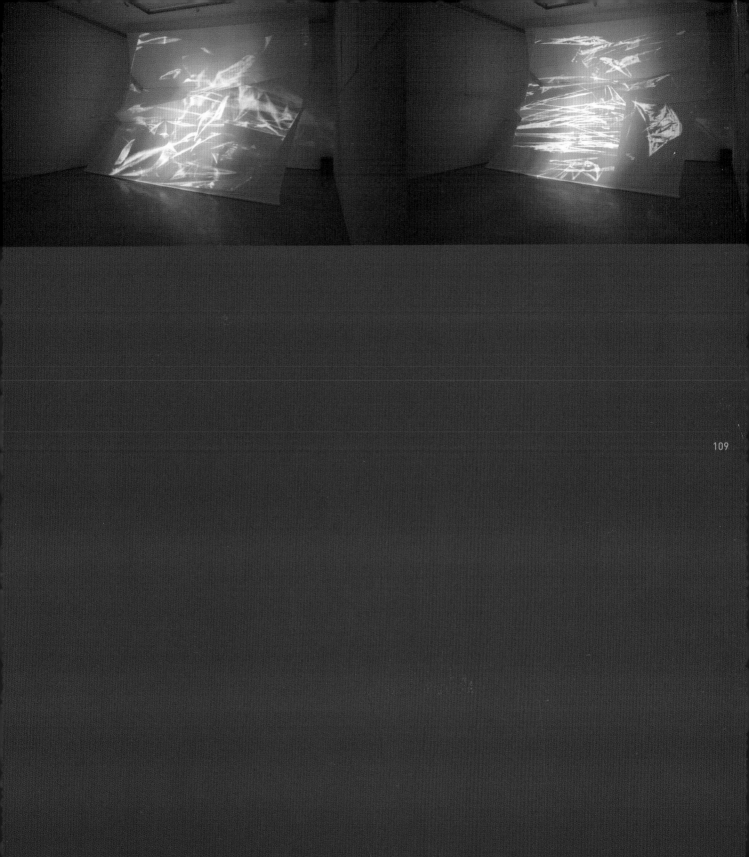

The texture map, which essentially incorporates an image, text, or pattern overlaid or superimposed onto any computer-generated surface, construct, or image, reveals an array of potential readings and misreadings. It is similar to the traditions of collage or filmic montage, yet it distinguishes itself significantly in that it creates an entity composed of distinct yet morphologically integrated components and reveals inherent structure and possibility.

Architexturing Copenhagen

STEEL PARK INTERVENTION

PROCEDURES

(01) The city plan of Copenhagen is subjected to an external and impartial device, isolating various unexpected sites for possible intervention. Each of these "overlooked" territories contains latent programs and architectures that may be brought to the fore by means of a series of chance texture-mapping operations.

(02) Texture maps are formulated according to certain "field operations" retrieved by combining labyrinthine mathematical strategies. Each resultant construct is integrated within the aerial surveillance photographs of the various sites determined by the overlay of the Universal Transverse Mercator grid.

(03) These combined images are interpreted to reveal potential strategies for architectural interventions within the residual territories made apparent through aerial surveillance.

(04) Programs are integrated through another set of chance operations. These sites contain an immanent architecture that might, through a slight adjustment of one's comprehension, become appreciated as actual sites of spectacle (i.e., tourist attractions).

THREE NEW URBAN INTERVENTIONS

(01) Bridges for bicycles and pedestrians cross the famous Copenhagen canals. This is a strategy for negotiating the entire canal system of the city, allowing boats to pass beneath and pedestrians and cyclists to meander above.

(02) An existing landscape of warehouses and empty storage buildings on a pier are converted into a topiary landscape and structures cut through to reveal galleries, museums, and other public spaces.

(03) An abandoned industrial lot is transformed into a park constructed entirely of horizontal and tilted steel plates, creating a new landscape on the outskirts of the city.

CANAL LATTICE BRIDGE STRUCTURES

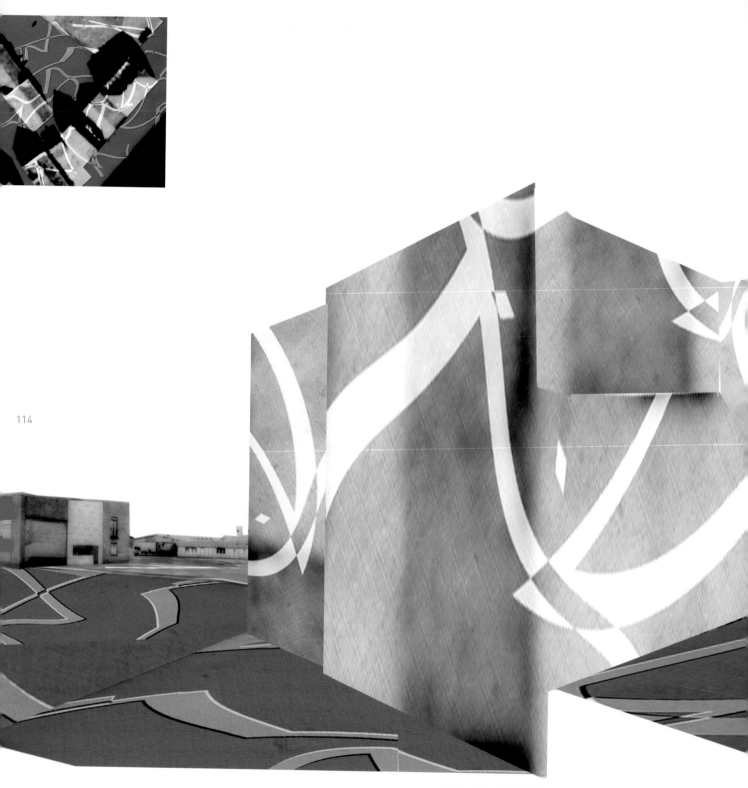

114

PIER INTERVENTION

Experimental Music Theater
Graz, Austria

At the center of this proposal is an affinity between physical presence (architecture) and ephemeral construct (music). This play between natural orders and manufactured artifice is accompanied by the sounds and actions that seep into and from the building's interiority. This music theater is not only a functional container but also an adjustable apparatus, a spatial and sonic instrument deployed at the scale of the city. The cuts, fissures, and topological surfaces that form this work allude not only to the architecture of musical artifacts (piano keys, brass valves, reeds, strings), but also to the abstract mathematical entities and relationships by which sound is formed. The articulations of facade, roof, and fenestration are at once as cacophonous as they are harmonious, reverberating with both the city and the creative processes within.

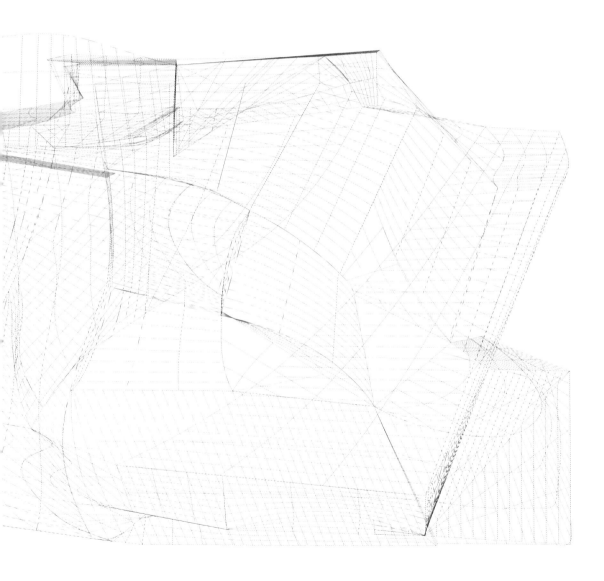

The music theater consists of three distinct components wrapped in an articulated shell. The entrance foyer is voluminous and transparent, a public gathering space where students, performers, and audience meet to discuss and anticipate the events that are to take place. The second area, immediately accessible from the entrance foyer, is the "black-box" music theater. This area, where performances, rehearsals, and events unfold, is versatile and fully transformable in terms of seating configurations, acoustic baffles, reconfiguration of stage platforms, and the control over light,

views, and external sound. A third component includes rehearsal studios, storage areas, and workshops, while a fourth comprises the dressing rooms and ancillary offices. These components are envisioned not so much as purely utilitarian and functional but as adapted specifically to enable the events that take place here. The workshops as well as the rehearsal studios admit generous amounts of natural light from skylights above. The dressing room areas and rehearsal studios feature ample lounge space within the circulation space, reinforcing the idea of the music theater

as a social venue where ideas and experiences are shared. The public aspects of what are usually private areas are made manifest through subtle and chance views of the work and storage areas, while inadvertent sounds escape into the realm of the city.

The black-box theater can be closed off from the circulation areas around its perimeter to become a completely self-contained environment. The sliding panels that enclose and delineate the theater may be opened or removed so it can become

part of the peripheral zones that surround it. The theater interior engages both the street and the adjacent park through fissures and cuts that permit views out to the city beyond. A rehearsal might be heard by pedestrians passing by, as is often the case in Graz; or a glimpse through the theater to the park beyond may provide a backdrop to the interior performance.

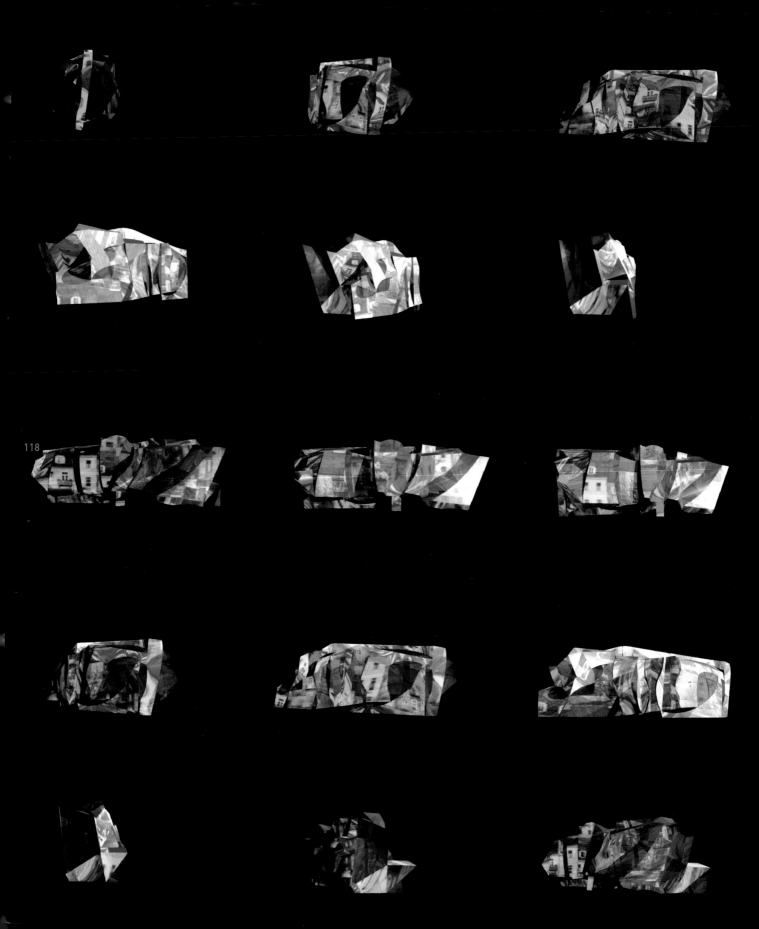

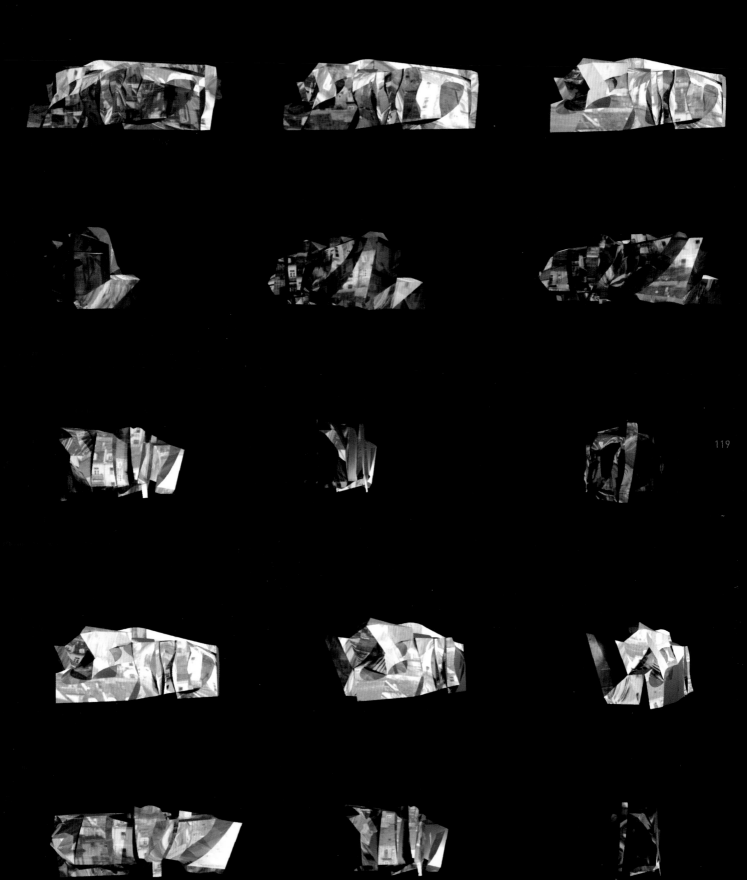

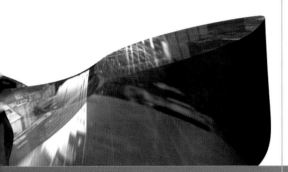
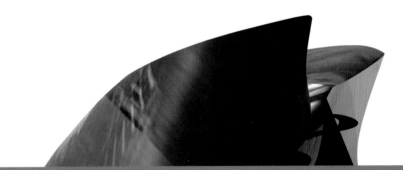

Technology Culture Museum
New York, New York

The end of the twentieth century saw the proliferation and profound impact of information technology, dematerialization, and simulation on all aspects of culture. In particular, museums and other places of cultural dissemination have been grappling with what constitutes experience, aesthetics, and perhaps most explicitly, reality. The Technology Culture Museum as conceived by Asymptote will house what is essentially the output of late modernity, the result of a trajectory through the twentieth century and a fluctuating notion of progress and innovation.

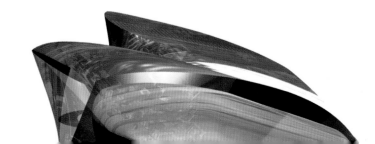

This museum follows a trajectory that has its origins in the beginning of the modern age, with the advent of buildings such as the Crystal Palace for the 1851 Great Exposition. Early Machine Age architecture expressed the anticipation of a coming century in which technological prowess and innovation would be the standards by which to measure progress. Today we stand at another threshold, one where technology is no longer manifest in mechanical objects and physical artifacts: this is a period of simulations, virtualization, bits, and disappearances. What was once the providence of world fairs and exposition grounds and later migrated into the realm of technology fairs and convention centers has now been relocated to the space of the museum. This trajectory has

brought the technological artifact from a world of experimentation through to utility, commodity, and finally, display and enshrinement. In the late 1980s the Fiat factory in Turin, Italy, was transformed from a once-thriving place that fabricated vehicles into a minimal museum housing a collection of Bugatis. In recent years the San Francisco Museum of Modern Art has transformed its design and architecture galleries into a place where tents, bicycles, and Sony Walkmans sit side by side with Eames furniture and icons of modern art. In New York, the Museum of Modern Art used its sculpture garden to display an eclectic mix of contemporary automobiles; and the Solomon R. Guggenheim Museum used its famous ramps for an important exhibition on the art of the motorcycle.

These events have made explicit a tendency at the end of the twentieth century for museums to treat the technological objects that surround us as important works of "art."

The Technology Culture Museum is a hybrid structure merging a convention-center typology with the utility of a hangar structure, and the public event programming of sports stadia with museum programming. The resulting building is a 300-meter-long structure located off piers 9 and 11 in the East River along the edge of lower Manhattan. The building's vast interior is designed to accommodate large-scale expositions, media events, and public spectacles as well as more intimately scaled events and exhibitions.

The museum's primary focus is technology and its relation to the human condition from the end of the twentieth century into the twenty-first century. Visitors will be able to experience the aesthetic qualities and cultural relevancy of technological innovation in much the same manner that they became accustomed to experiencing art in museum settings throughout the later part of the twentieth century.

The Technology Culture Museum articulates and makes explicit the convergence of art, technology, culture, and commodity. One potential exhibition might be a carefully curated collection of objects used during the Cold War, such as missiles, spy satellites, and nuclear submarines. As the world becomes increasingly mediated by technological innovations it seems as if the museum has become the last refuge of the real, understood in terms of physicality — as if the "real" is something to be contained and entombed. The museum's architecture becomes both the frame and affirmation of this notion of reality.

The architectural assembly protrudes from Manhattan into the East River and exemplifies a type of urban intervention perhaps more in keeping with Pacific Rim models of expansion, where buildings act as prostheses to the urban density. An internal space that qualifies as perhaps the largest container of public events and exhibitions in the world is framed by a long-span steel structure designed and constructed using computer modeling and fabrication techniques to achieve its fluid forms. The skin is entirely clad in "video" signals, utilizing a hybrid material that melds LCD technologies with cladding technologies to create a building envelope capable of broadcasting digital signals across the whole surface. The "liquid" presence of this architecture suggests a structure grafted onto the city's ephemeral and mediated condition. The museum is part of the city of Manhattan, where the duality of hypermediation and physical presence — a condition of perpetual flux — is explicit.

Kyoto Multimedia Center
Kyoto, Japan

Along with Western contemporary culture, technological innovation, and media and
entertainment, Japan has now embraced another import, the "Edutainment" industry.
Spawned by Silicon Valley and Hollywood, this industry demonstrates its application most
obviously in mall culture, Internet commerce, theme parks, and urban development.
Kyoto is a city that is at once as traditional and mystical as it is forward looking. Here, the
unique mix of culture, science, and history are bracketed on one side by Shinto temples
and gardens and on the other by avant-garde theater and performance art.

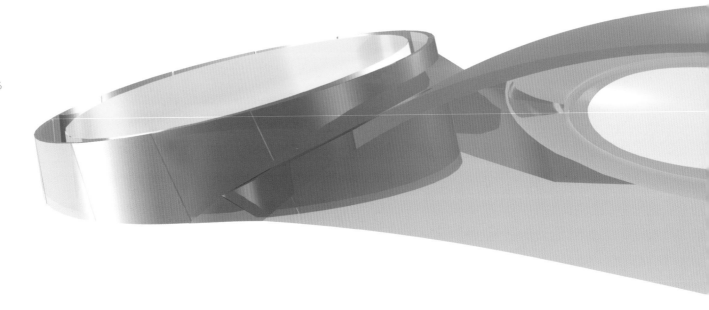

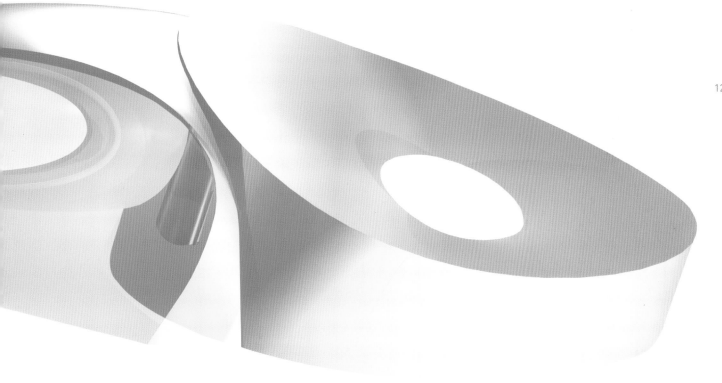

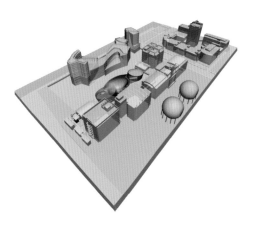

The Japanese appropriation of this Edutainment industry will, like so many other Western influences, undoubtedly be tempered and distinguished by its Asian translation and assimilation into Japanese culture. The Kyoto Edutainment Center brings together various aspects from the worlds of media, entertainment, and culture, each integrated into a publicly accessible facility in the heart of Kyoto. In this complex, Japan's first Edutainment Museum, broadcasting facilities for high-density television, multimedia production workshops, and a "black-box" technology theater coexist as a single facility.

The architecture of the Kyoto Edutainment Center melds culture, commerce, and technology in a complex where public event and spectacle are manifest and programmed. The building is designed around the notion that the forms and tectonics emerging from our familiarity with computer-designed objects and images can yield new architectural forms and assemblies. Automobiles, Web pages, and domestic objects (athletic shoes, toasters, home computers) form a landscape based on digital manufacture and aesthetics. Ubiquitous marketing and advertising cement our familiarity with

these things. Also important are inherent discrepancies between function, form, meaning, and ideology, which, while blurred, form the basis of the Edutainment Industry. The Edutainment Museum and other facilities planned here will exist as physical architectural presences within this condition of ambiguity. The curvilinear forms, material juxtapositions (the result of texture mapping), and fluidity of functions and programs all anticipate our evolving condition.

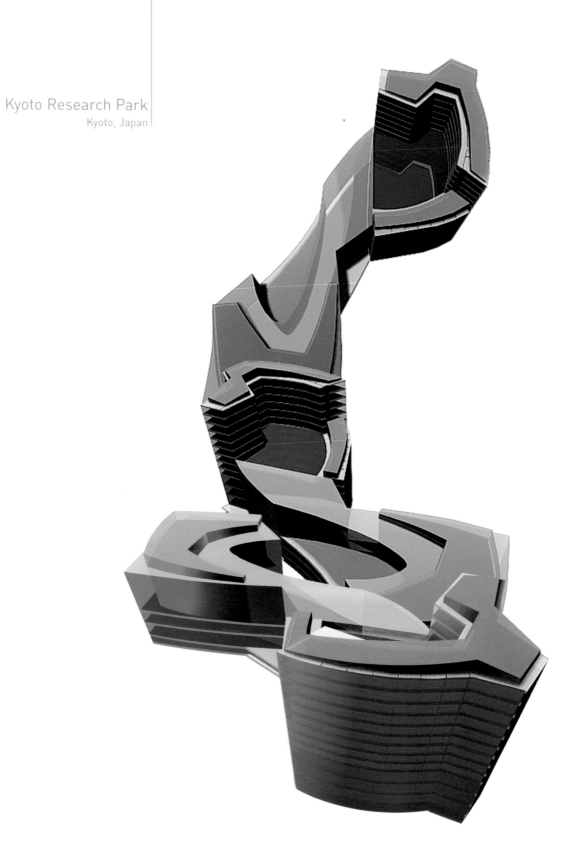

The shift toward technological enterprises within Japanese commerce prompted this proposal for a building complex that includes lab and office space for various multimedia research groups as well as new public amenities. The project consists of a collection of buildings on a tract of industrially zoned land close to Kyoto's urban center. The architecture responds to several conditions imposed on this building complex. First, these facilities are urban entities, accommodating the influx of people from Kyoto's city center as well as visitors from abroad. This called for a high-profile architectural solution that would reconcile the deep-seated traditions of Japan's oldest city, Kyoto, with the aspirations of the Japanese to embrace new technologies.

The new multimedia research facilities include fiber-optic networked office space and hotel, a Sega game center, virtual reality cinemas, retail areas, and a technologically advanced health club. Also on the site is a multimedia performance space designed specifically for theater and events that depend on a high-technology facility. This project offered a unique opportunity to merge typical business models with cultural and entertainment facilities in a single complex of buildings. The notion of mixing business with pleasure and diversion, so important to the modern Japanese way of life, was critical to the planning and conceptualization of this project.

The architectural assembly of the buildings reflects the study and deliberate quotation of architectural elements and motifs within ancient Japanese traditions. Certain geomantic principles, coupled with notions of solidity, transparency, and massing, influence a landscape that meanders between the massive transparent volumes of the buildings. These new structures accommodate and reframe the existing research facilities by creating interstitial areas and landscapes between them. The use of quotations and strategies from traditional Japanese architecture and garden design resulted in architecture that is subdued and wholly integrated while still remaining quite large in scale. Formal principles joined with other themes, mainly those of translucency, luminosity, and color. The glass-encased buildings are conventional in their curtain-wall construction, yet they are equipped with electronic glass panels that change density and coloration. Computer systems count the users occupying the building at any given moment, processing and managing data that is transferred to the glass panes to control color density and hue. As a result, the facades are constantly altering according to the building's interior life. As the buildings fill with people, they move toward complete transparency, and as they empty the glass turns particular translucent colors. The modulated surface coloration and density effect a unique visual rhythm within the city's own rhythm. The architecture itself, in continual transformation, assumes an "intelligence" as a spectacle visible to Kyoto's inhabitants and visitors.

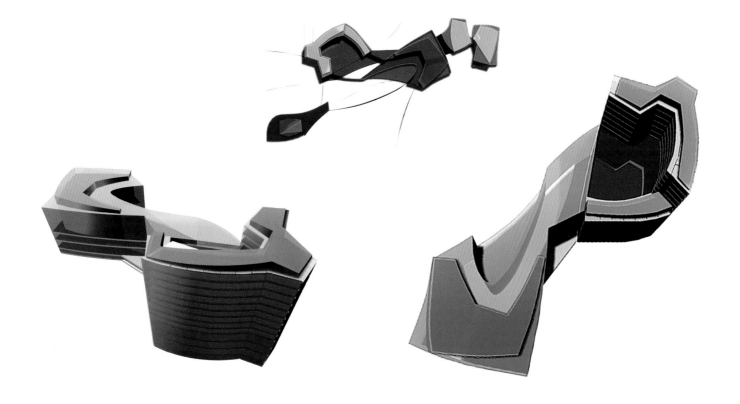

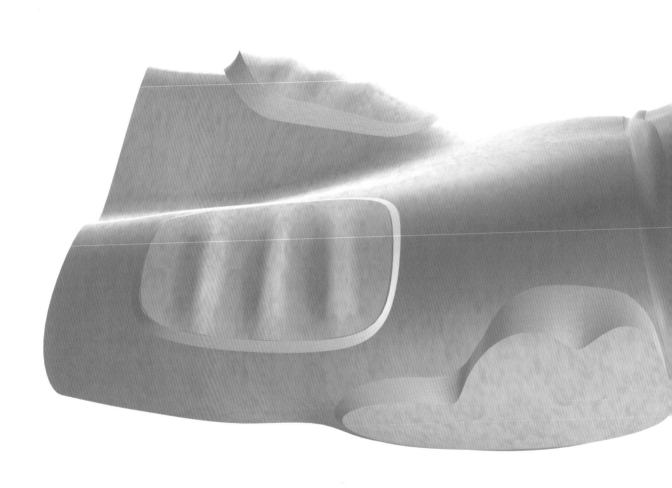

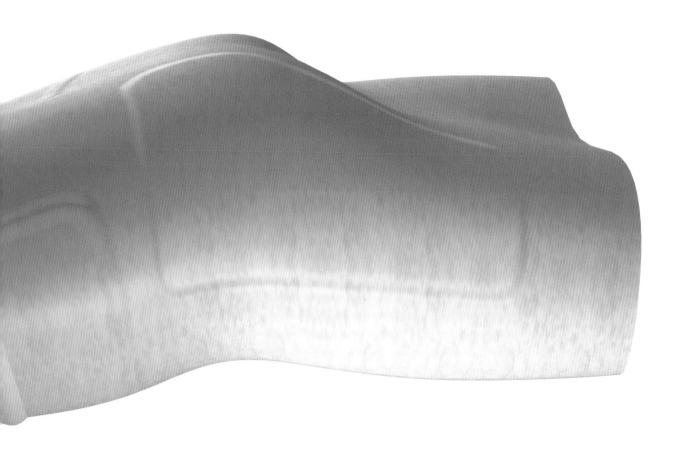

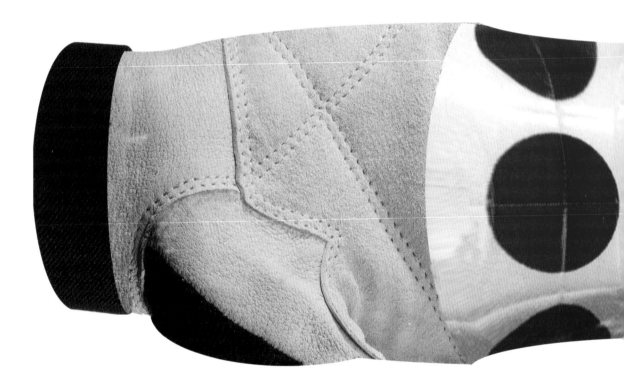

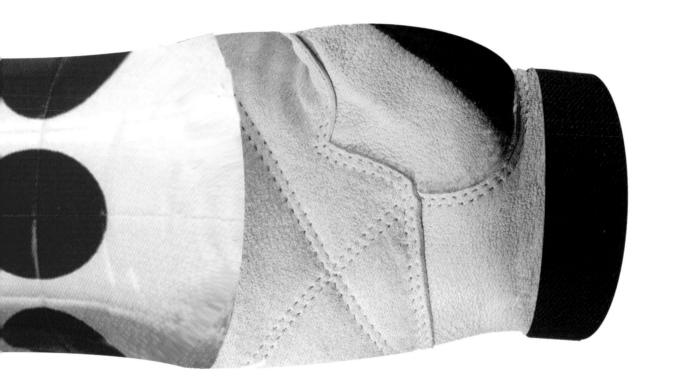

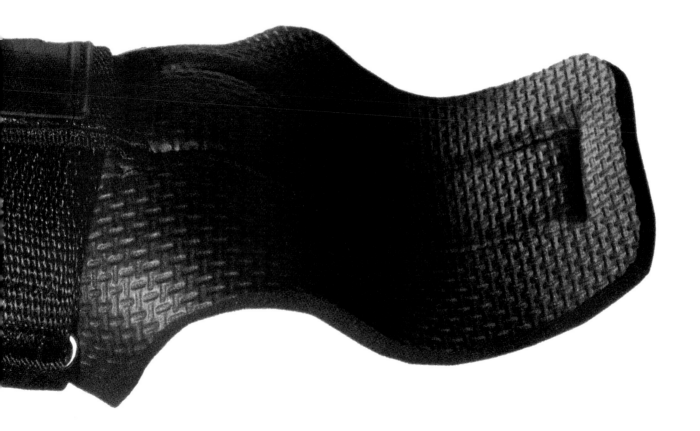

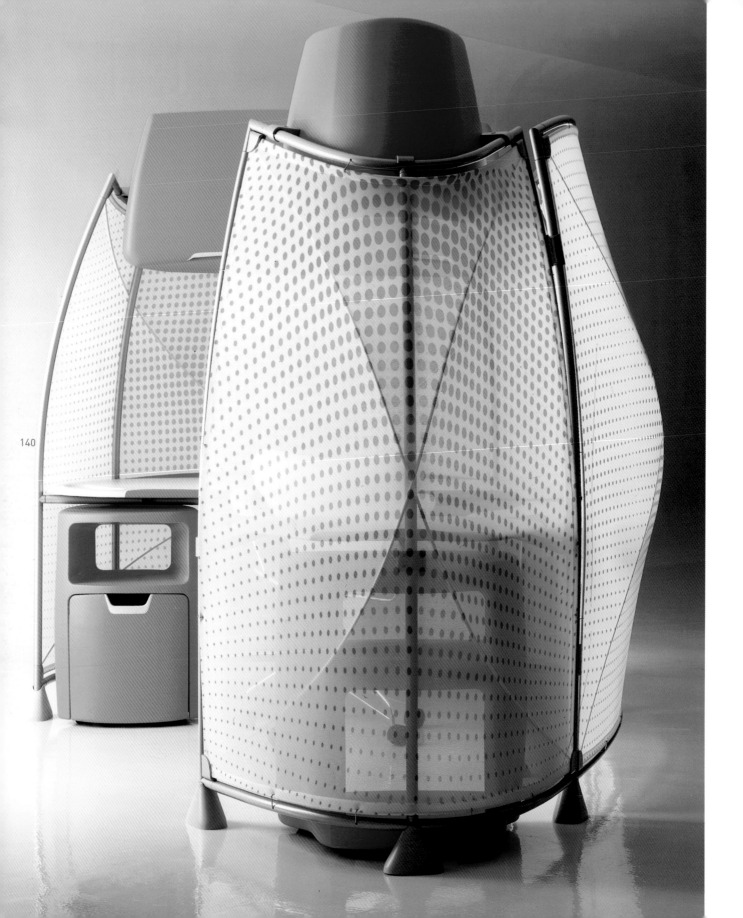

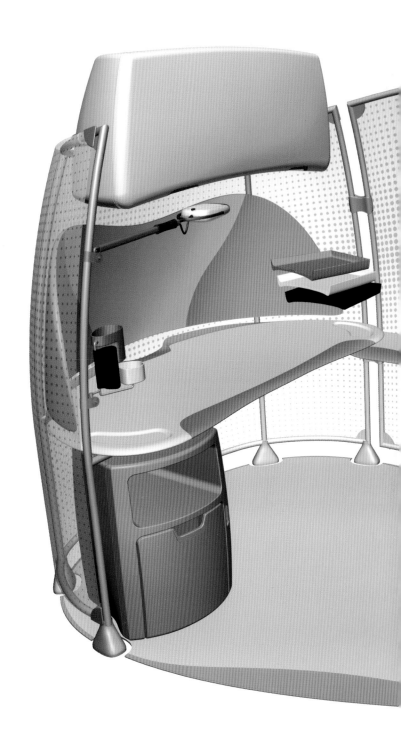

Knoll A3 Furniture System

From the outset, the Knoll A3 project
was a complete revaluation and overhaul
of the conventional — and some would
say outmoded — office cubicle. With our
background in architecture as opposed
to industrial design, Asymptote was
predisposed to take an initial approach
that was spatial and environmental rather
than primarily object-driven. The project
was seen as a valuable opportunity to
rethink the dynamics of the office landscape: How do people interact in quasi-
wireless, digitally equipped environments?
How can one have a sense of privacy while
also feeling like part of a larger community? What are the new emotionally
charged forms and materials that we
surround ourselves with on a daily basis?
How can these be employed to create
vibrant and interesting work environments
and furnishings? How can a desire for
versatility and flexibility be accommodated
while at the same time maintaining a high
level of efficiency? Can this be achieved
while still bringing a sense of order and
dignity to our workspaces?

SINGLE WORKSTATION

MIRRORED

ROTATED 90⁰

ROTATED 120⁰

ROTATED 120⁰

ROTATED 120⁰

ROTATED 120⁰

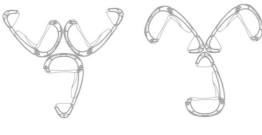

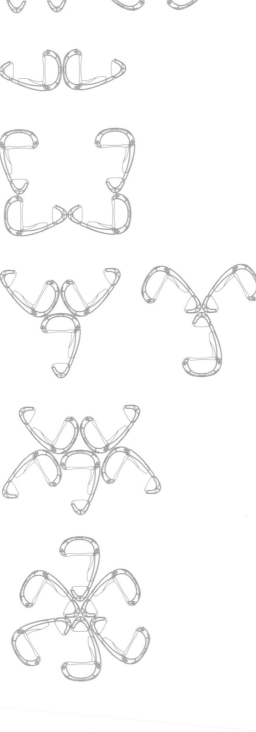

One of the most important skills of architectural design is the ability to think on multiple scales simultaneously. Here this meant considering space from the scale of the individual to group cluster arrangements to the entire workspace. Knoll A3 is designed to be a highly flexible and compelling new type of office system, one that allows for modularity within the individual workstation and encourages new ways of planning and implementing entire office environments. At the overall planning scale the beautiful arabesque qualities of the cluster arrangements and layout configurations create a new "office-scape," an antidote to the relentless, monotonous interior conditions that often result from planning with conventional systems. The use of curvilinear geometry also affords the opportunity for planners and designers to create alcoves, impromptu gathering spots, breakout spaces, and meeting areas, all of which contribute to an active, imaginative, and engaged workplace community.

The A3 system is easy to install and can be recombined and reconfigured to respond to behavioral, technical, and architectural needs. It was imperative that the new workstation no longer feel impersonal and "machined" but rather become a desirable, human-scaled place to inhabit. In other words, both the physical spaces we occupy and the ways in which we occupy them should be reconsidered as we move into the future. The curvilinear geometry of the A3 system humanizes the office spaces we occupy. One's workspace should feel comfortable in terms of the way it surrounds the body and accommodates its movement. With this in mind, Asymptote asked why our environments so often tend to be rigid and rectilinear, and provided a solution in which the movement of the body in space describes a geometry of sweeps and curves.

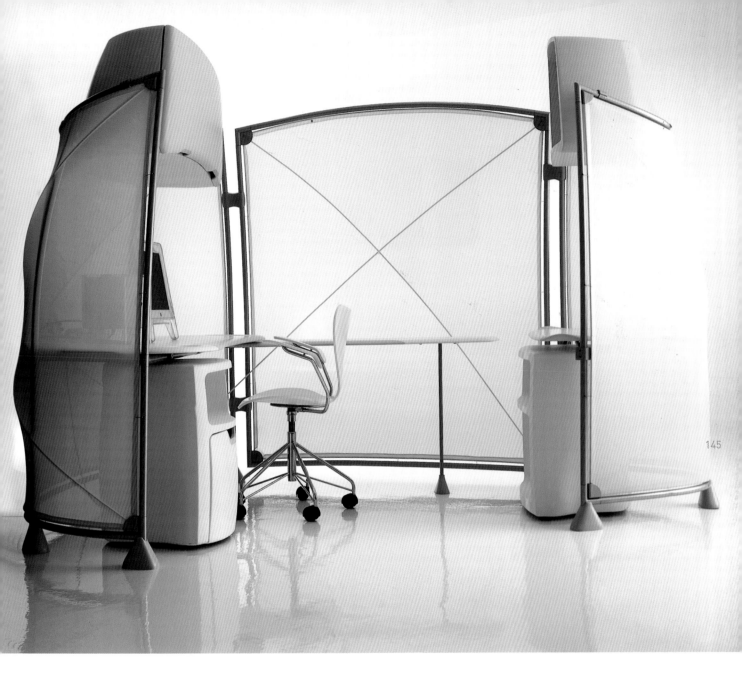

In addition to fulfilling feelings of well being, the workspace must also respond to the needs for privacy and community. Asymptote did not see these needs as incompatible. The deliberate gaps in the A3 enclosure and the use of semi-transparent screens help achieve this response to combined needs. The resulting feeling of lightness further contributes to the sense of well being. Asymptote turned to a number of other design sources for inspiration in creating A3. For instance, since we wished to create an environment that fit with the body, we considered sports apparel and sports gear as a means of protecting the body and allowing it to feel secure and comfortable. We found this to be an interesting analog when we realized that a large number of advertising campaigns seemed to offer images of sports activities and the outdoors as countermeasures to the negative qualities associated with conventional cubicle work environments. Images of activities such camping or mountain biking became vivid symbols of escape from the dismal space of the conventional office and the banal routine of work. These sports inspired the forms and materials of A3 and constituted a new kind of language.

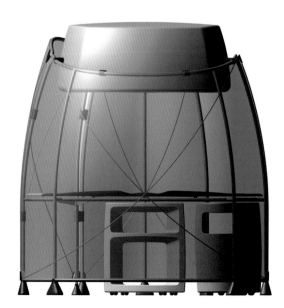

The A3 system is also very attentive to technology within the workplace. The product is designed with the recognition that we are increasingly moving toward wireless and transient types of environments where the workplace is used in a more dynamic, freeform way, evolving from technological potential and innovations. That said, today's workplace still contains considerable wiring. The cable manage-ment system for the Knoll A3 is multifac-eted and versatile enough to accommodate our wired present as well as a wireless future. Many new manufacturing tech-niques and materials were used in the project, including injection-molded plastics and newly engineered textiles for the screens. By streamlining the quantity of materials used in the workstation, using a high percentage of recycled material, and facilitating the separation of materials for future recycling, Asymptote was able to create not only a more humane and functional work environment but also one that better respects the natural environment.

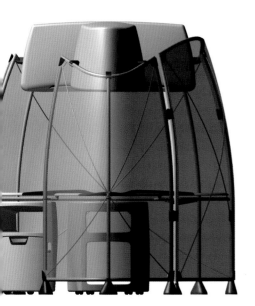

A3 frame

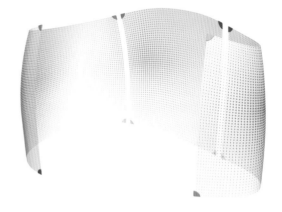

screen

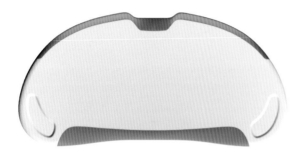

Arc work surface

Surf return

Filez file pedestal

Tript pedestal

power module

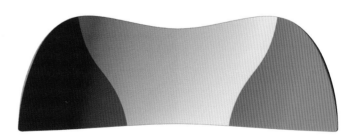

Visor

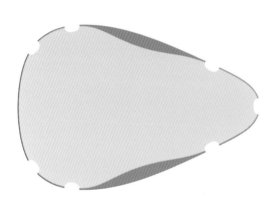

pad

Flipp lamp

Slipp work surface

Slipp table

small Aerial overhead

large Aerial overhead

Orbit cups

Scoop

The Guggenheim Center for Art and Technology focuses not only on technology but on interaction, digital media, and the new cultural tendencies inspired by such influences. This new venue, which will occupy the street level of the Solomon R. Guggenheim Museum's SoHo location in New York, fuses innovation and information with emerging cutting-edge technologies, culture, and commerce. The space engages not only local visitors but also a broader, technologically present global community.

The center is located in the uninterrupted through-block space that connects Broadway and Mercer streets, and contains three distinct programmatic elements. Primarily, it is a flagship venue for the Guggenheim.com enterprise, allowing people to visit and use a physical space in conjunction with the online cultural portal. Second, the center is dedicated to a new retail model, where exhibited objects of contemporary design are presented as "curated" merchandise available for purchase directly from the Guggenheim. Third, it is a new venue for showcasing and

featuring new media, video, and digital art within what has become known as "Silicon Alley" within the SoHo art precinct. The Guggenheim Virtual Museum and the Guggenheim.com initiatives are center-pieces for the Guggenheim's increased visibility in electronic space. Both projects symbolize the Guggenheim's commitment to and understanding of entirely new avenues for the merging of art, culture, and technology.

153

INSERTIONS: Five large-scale glass vitrines within the center of the space highlight selected objects of sophisticated and high-quality contemporary design. These vitrines, which can house very large objects such as automobiles, are designed in such a way that contained objects will seem to float in an atmosphere of light. Showcasing these curated objects makes evident the overlap between cultural display and commercial promotion, between art and commodity. In effect, this overlap is the unacknowledged undercurrent of many contemporary museum practices.

INTERACTION: The north wall of the space, which is highly visible to pedestrians on Broadway, will function as the main interactive component. The wall contains fifteen 20-inch, high-definition, flat-screen monitors, each capable of high-speed Web access. The touch-screen interface allows visitors to survey the Guggenheim.com site and all of its content. The monitors are to be tethered to the "sculpted" architecture of the north wall by means of moveable and adjustable supports and can be used for individual or group viewing. Through the use of technologies such as live-

camera feeds, information-gathering and dispersion software, and online retail and auction capabilities, the Guggenheim.com Interactive Wall is a provocative component of the museum's global image.

...mprises a video wall. ...rface not only impacts the ...y but also becomes an ...elivery system for a wide ...rom live performances, ...posia to film and video- ...e new video wall will be ...opposite the stairs lead- ...s on the upper floors and

Koolhaas–designed Prada store next door. This placement increases the drama and visibility of the wall and makes use of the stairs to provide ample space for gathering, seating, and the viewing of various events and presentations.

VIDEO-GATEWAY: The Mercer Street side of the renovated space accommodates the

resolution, flat-screen computer monitors, capable of displaying extremely high-definition streaming images. The surface can be programmed for a wide range of content to function as a multimedia and Web-art showcase as well as a digital billboard. During opening hours the video wall is a dynamic visual backdrop to the interior space; when the center is closed

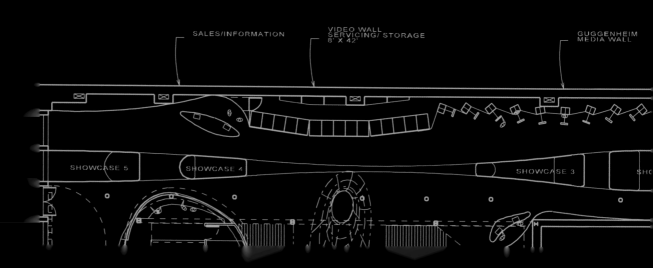

SALES/INFORMATION

VIDEO WALL
SERVICING/ STORAGE
8' X 42'

GUGGENHEIM
MEDIA WALL

SHOWCASE 5

SHOWCASE 4

SHOWCASE 3

SHO

the screen pivots into a position visible from Mercer Street. Located beneath the west stairway is the ArtLab, a digital studio facility where visiting artists can work in video production and editing on the premises. The ArtLab, which allows visitors to observe the various processes at work within, also serves as a video DJ booth during public events.

THE VIRTUAL MUSEUM: The Guggenheim Virtual Museum (GVM) will be implemented as a real-time "virtual artifact" for public viewing within the Center for Art and Technology. A large suspended volume contains and displays the GVM as a holographic image at the intersection of the stairs to the upper-level galleries and the passage into the adjacent store. The rotating, constantly changing images

modulate according to the GVM's real-time Internet activities and the occupancy tabulation it has at any given moment. The GVM's "actual" presence in the space provides a visually compelling element and locates an actual place for the Guggenheim's Virtual Museum.

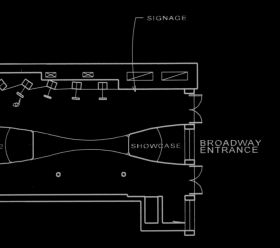

FLIGHT	DESTINATION	SCHED	EST
AZ 605	MILAN/MALPENSA	1720	1721
NN 8705	MILAN/MALPENSA	1720	1720
AF 011	PARIS - COG	1730	1730
OL 8261	PARIS - COG	1730	1730
OA 412	ATHENS - NELLINIKON	1735	173
TK 1492	ISTANBUL - ATATURK	1815	1815
OS 502	VIENNA	1835	1035

mike

Lounge
A,B,C,D

The future of cities and the ways of corporate culture are inextricably linked. The airport is today a surrogate city-space equipped with all the attributes of urbanism yet at the same time hygienically insulated and controlled. In response to the remarkable ease of global movement and a modern nomadic culture engendered by multinational corporations and air travel, a new urbanism is emerging from the hybridized condition of the airport. Schipol in Amsterdam and Heathrow in London are examples of highly engineered spaces, not only for air traffic but also for shopping, meeting, and entertaining. The advent of digital technologies has spawned in most business sectors two seemingly contradictory trends: long-distance communication by sophisticated electronic means, and a vast increase in travel and the need for face-to-face meetings. As businesses merge and grow around the globe, airports have attempted to keep pace by offering executive business areas, lounges, places of worship, and a plethora of other features that at one time only real city space might have provided. These trends suggest that airports will transform into places that people not so much simply pass through but instead use and inhabit. Cities have historically evolved around trade routes and transportation nodes, including waterways, highways, and rail lines. In today's continually changing global corporate culture we are seeing the evolution of city space occurring in close proximity with — if not wedded to — new airport planning.

161

Copenhagen Airport: Welcome to the best
Airport you find a wide selection of well-kn
eight specialty shops. The eleven tax-free s
spirits, tobacco, and confectionery at some
can also visit our Christmas Shop at Nytorv.
meeting point with direct and nonstop c
A business address with an advanced telec
facilities. A highly attractive plaza, complet
mum public transport connection (direct a
depart for Munich every ten minutes). Singa
every transfer and transit need with facilities
travel woes. Whether you are looking for busi
thing for everyone. You can watch a free r
Theatrette. Passengers with five hours to sp
ister for a free two-hour sightseeing tour t
twenty-minute bumboat ride on the Singapo
Quay, and Clifford Pier.

opping center in the world. In Copenhagen

n international brands in no less than thirty-

s offer a wide range of perfume, cosmetics,

he lowest prices in Europe. In December you

unich International Airport: An international

ections to over two-hundred destinations.

mmunications infrastructure and conference

with restaurants, cafés, and shops. An opti-

ss to transit railway from the Forum; trains

re Changi Airport: Changi Airport serves your

nd convenient services that help to ease your

ss essentials or entertainment, there is some-

vie on a large screen at our 24-hour Movie

e before their next connecting flight can reg-

he city center, Raffles Landing site, and a

River, which has views of Boat Quay, Clarke

Dodger Stadium
Los Angeles, California

Straddling the line between the physical and the virtual, Asymptote's design for a new stadium for the Dodger baseball team proposes a fitting landmark for a city that hovers between artifice and reality. The project is envisioned as a state-of-the-art stadium with an air-supported roof constructed of new polymers and PVC fabrics that darken and lighten according to atmospheric conditions.

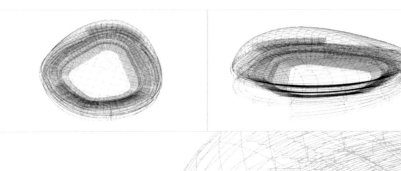

To shield fans from the area's poor air quality and from UV radiation, Asymptote envisioned an air-supported roof constructed of new polymers and PVC membrane fabrics. These new materials not only provide traditional protection from the elements but also achieve different levels of transparency as the composition of the air filtered into the inflatable structure is adjusted. This calibration modulates sunlight as required and creates complete transparency at night to accommodate helicopters equipped with television cameras circling above. This technology can also be used to program various graphics onto the roof surfaces to promote the host city, home team, corporate sponsors, or to affect patterns on the playing field by varying the levels of UV filtration. Circumscribing the interior of the stadium is a ticker that utilizes state-of-the-art imaging technologies for streaming text and video feeds simultaneously. The ticker displays electronically all game information in real time, including batting averages, speed of pitch, and other statistics. Circulation ramps are integrated into the building shell, while the concessions are located in a ring that continuously revolves around the perimeter of the seating structure.

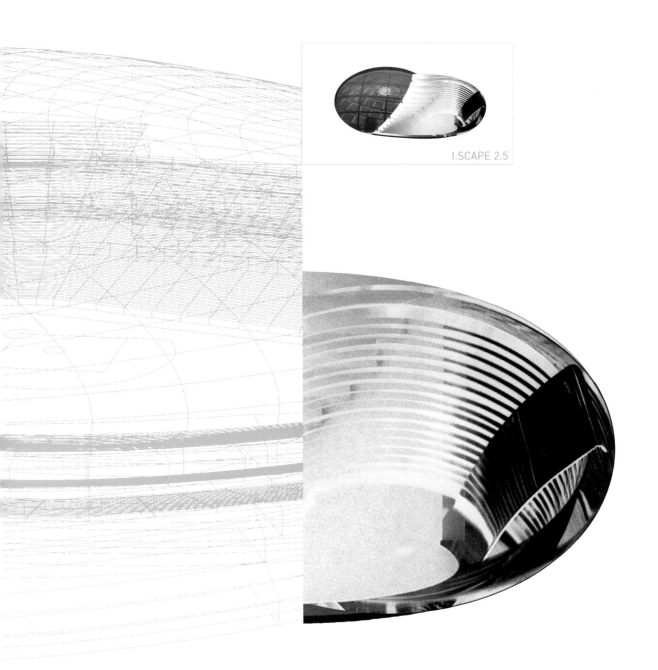

I.SCAPE 2.5

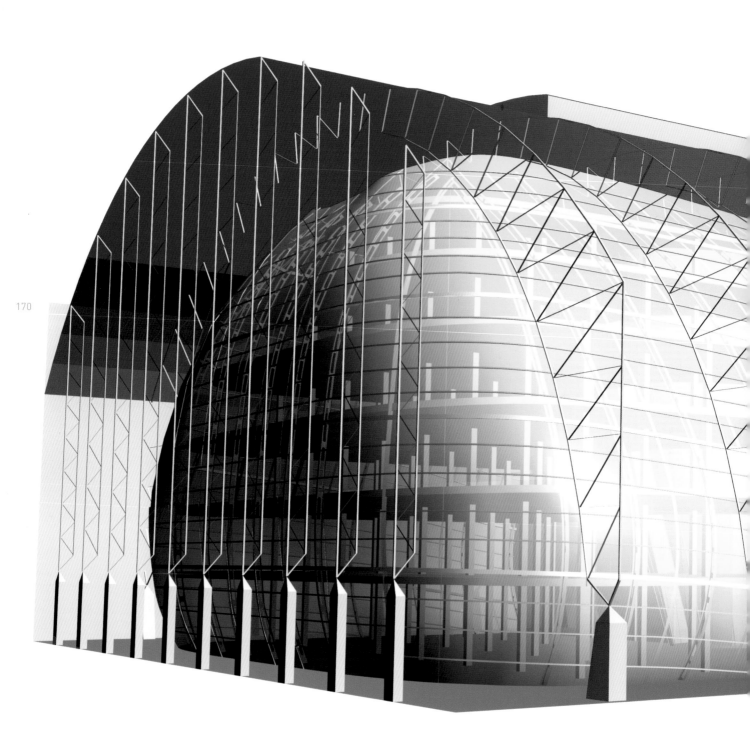

The Incubator
San Francisco, California

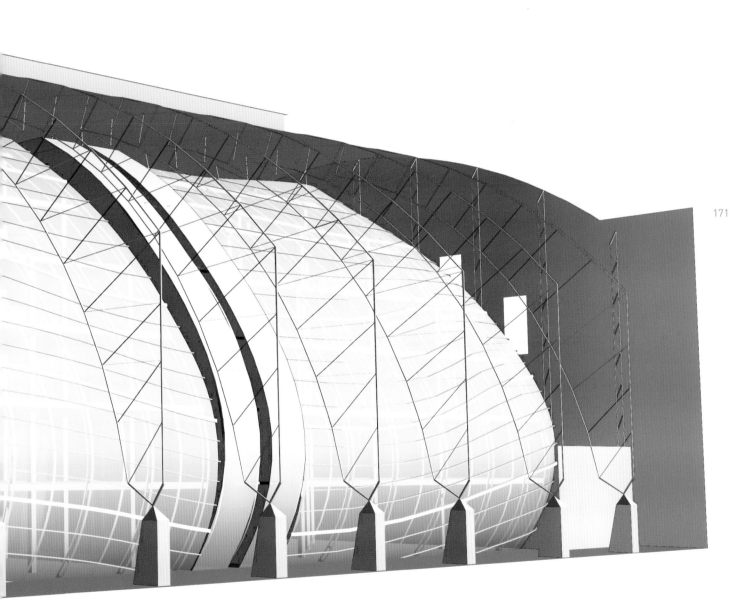

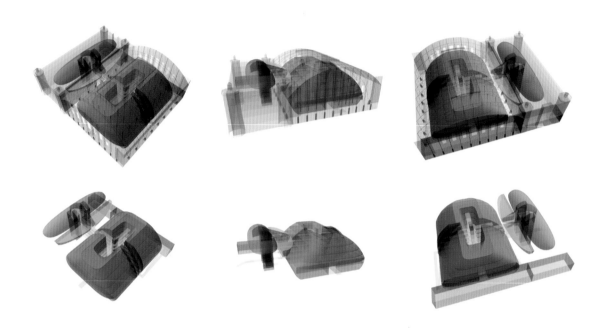

172

This new multimedia hub was proposed for the landmark Armory Building in San Francisco's Mission District. The project entails renovating existing office space and providing over 200,000 square feet of new leasable space for the growing e-industries within a structure formerly used as a parade ground. Asymptote proposed a new "building within a building" inside the impressive seven-story-high Armory.

Contrasting with and highlighting the existing nineteenth-century steel-truss structure would be a new facility incorporating the latest communication and digital technologies. The proposed building structure incorporates advanced fiber optics and light lens systems to maximize daylighting, and integrates all wiring, data feeds, and HVAC systems into the facade. Proposed tenant amenities, including a cafe, book-

store, fitness facilities, and "digital lounges," would be located in the open space surrounding and below the new structure and would also serve the local community. Public components such as digital training labs and exhibition galleries would contribute further to the community and offer opportunities for corporate-community partnerships.

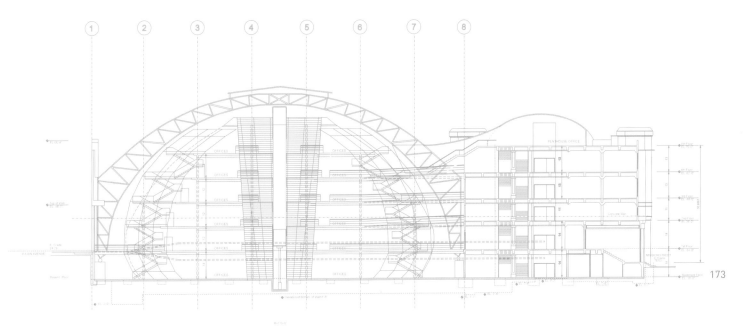

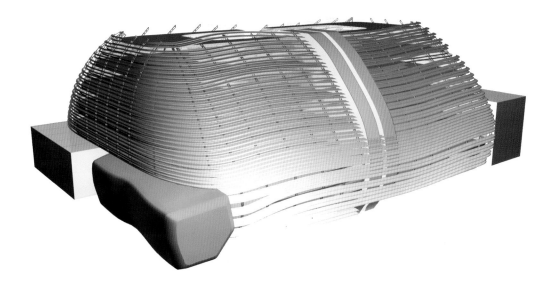

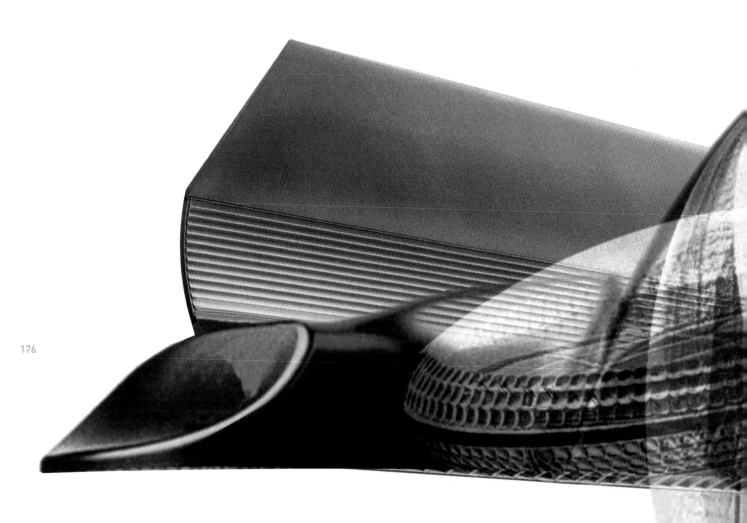

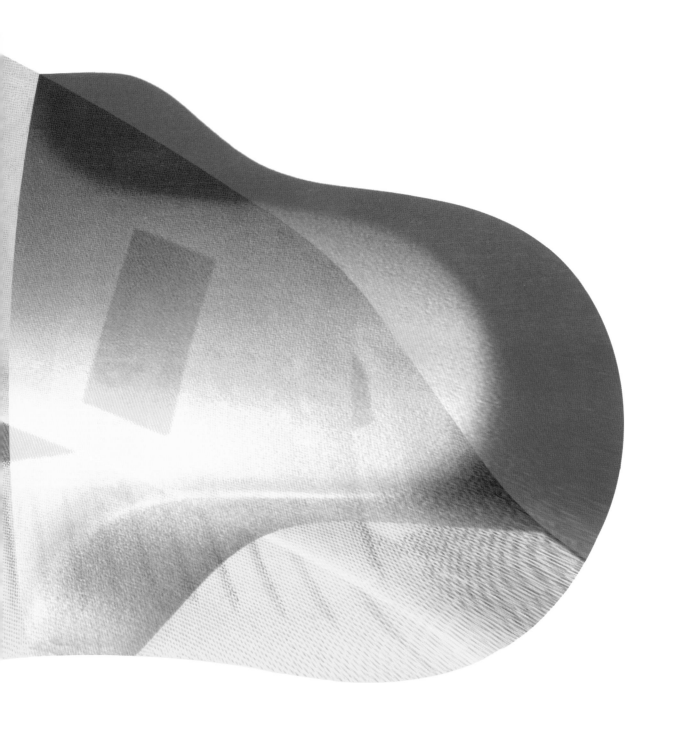

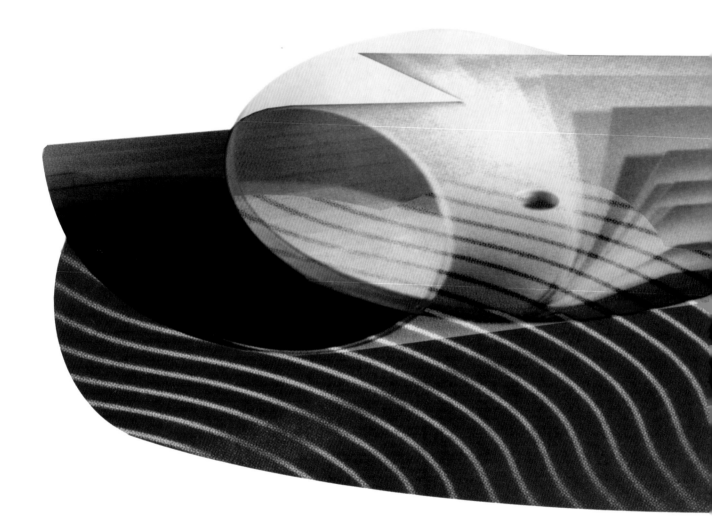

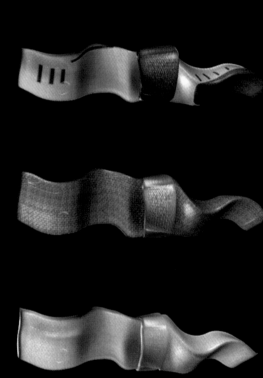

I.Scape Multiple

Asymptote's I.Scapes are discrete architectures provoked by and extrapolated from the proliferation of digitally manipulated imagery from mass culture, the media, and advertising.

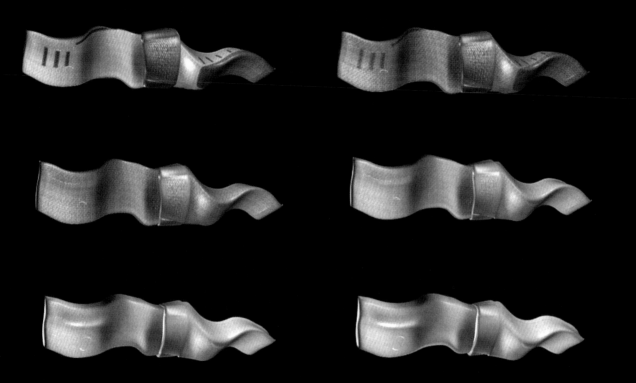

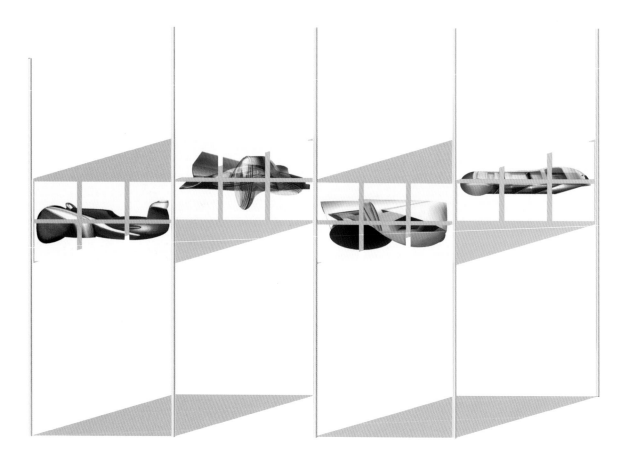

The I.Scapes derived from Asymptote's reading of the effect of the computer on culture, with particular focus on new formations of meaning and a revised understanding of what now constitutes spatiality. These territories, in which meaning is a substrate of seductive marketing, not only contain iconography and coding tied to demographics and desire but also underscore a critical fluctuation in present-day preoccupations and interests. The computer and the arsenal of digital implements it has spawned have impacted all aspects of the human condition.

The I.Scapes are neither appliance nor building. They are instead continuous and fluid tracings of uncanny resemblances. They fetishize mutation, distortion, and delirium, forming spaces fused with image. The forms are generated dynamically as both surface and volume, recalling the works of Frederick Kiesler, Hermann Finsterlin, Andrea Bloc, and other seekers of endless space. The choreographed assemblies meander through channels of possibility and familiarity, arriving by chance at unforeseen orders. They are at one moment body, the next object, then metal, then plastic, at once a complex geometry and an absolute flatness.

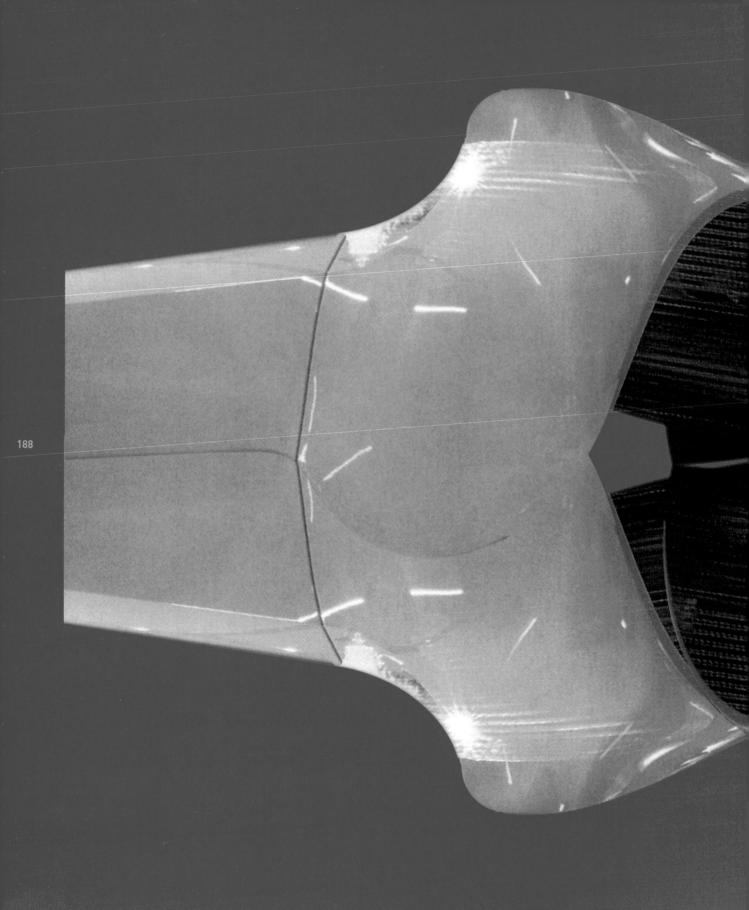

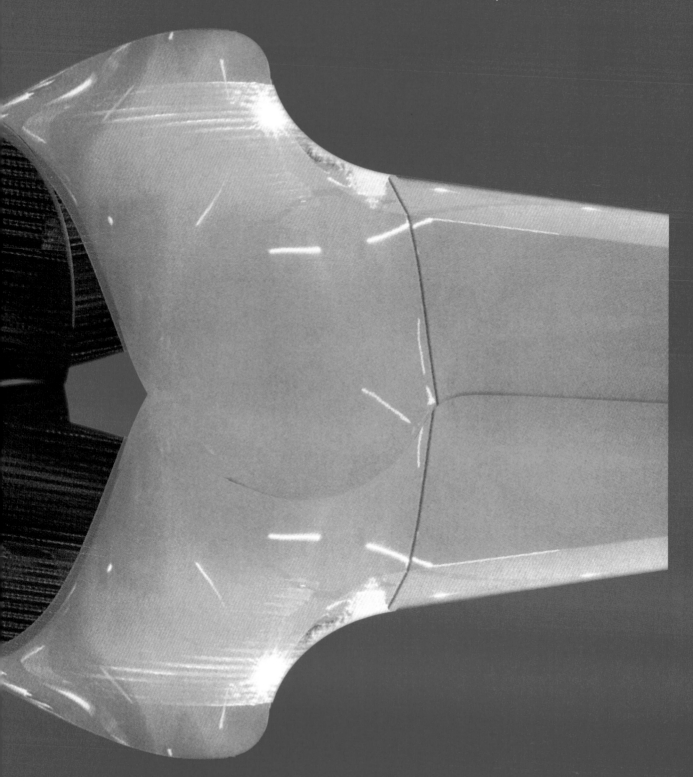

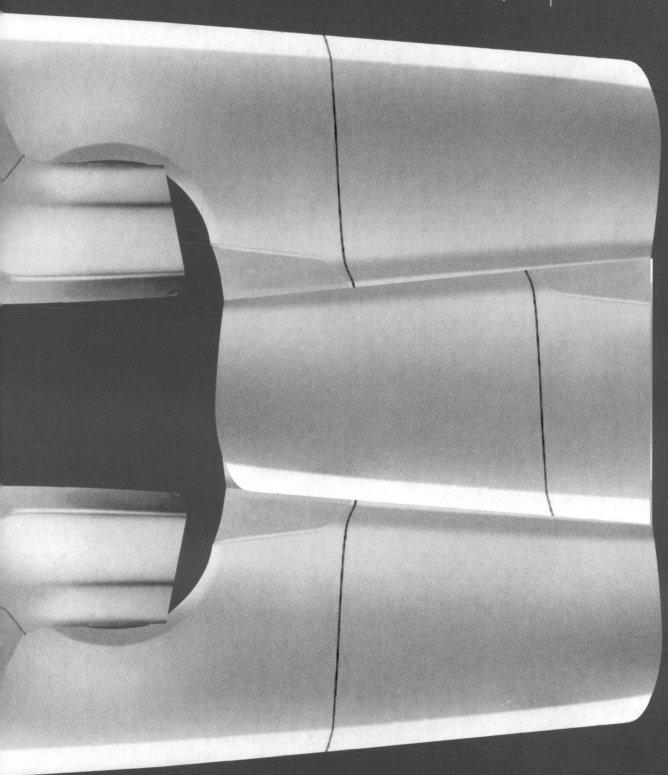

192

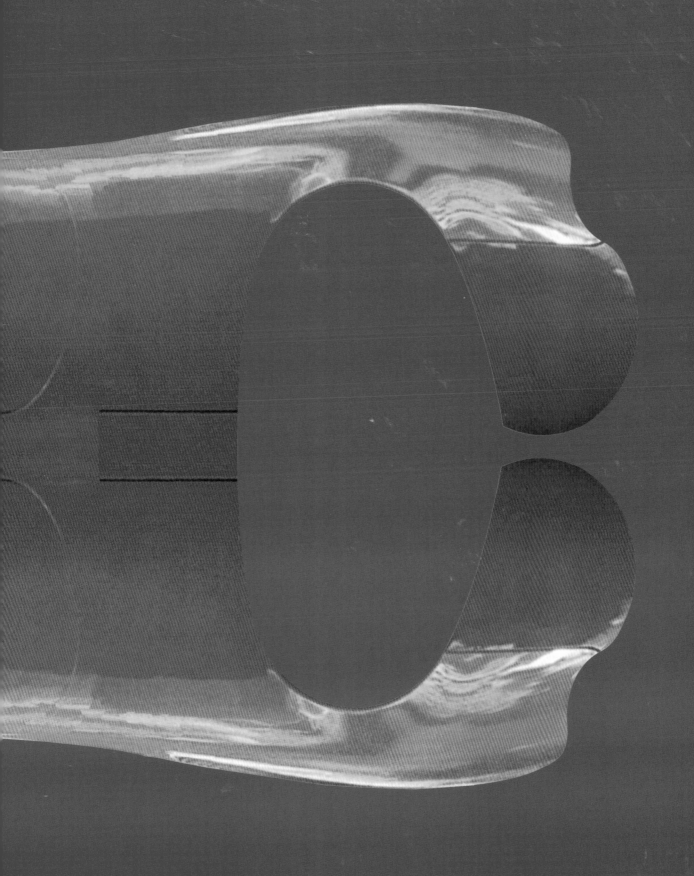

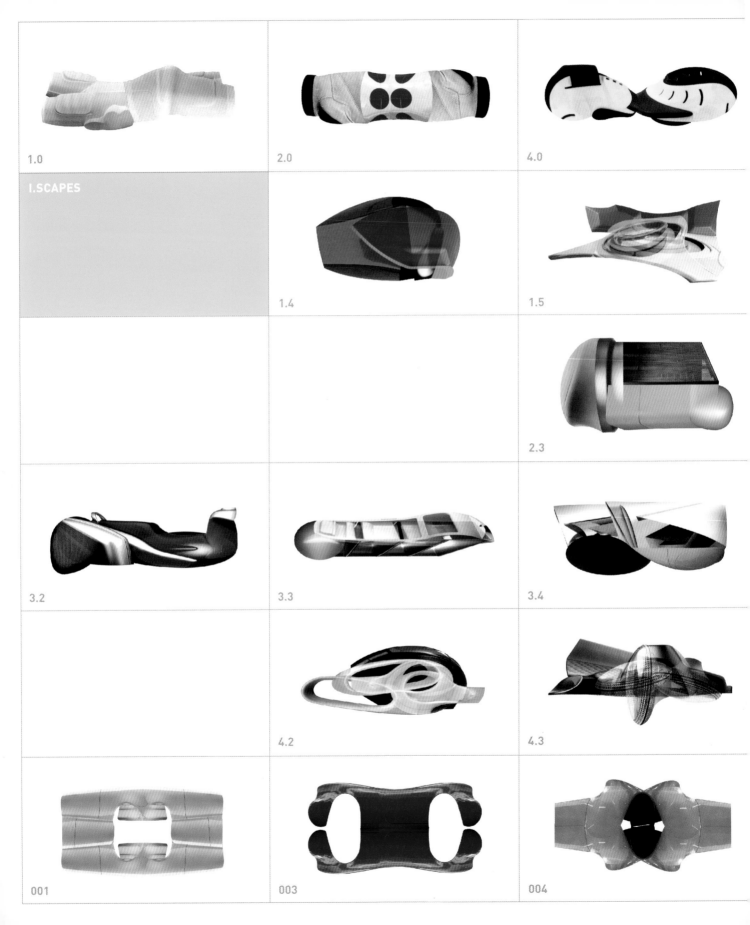

1.0

2.0

4.0

I.SCAPES

1.4

1.5

2.3

3.2

3.3

3.4

4.2

4.3

001

003

004

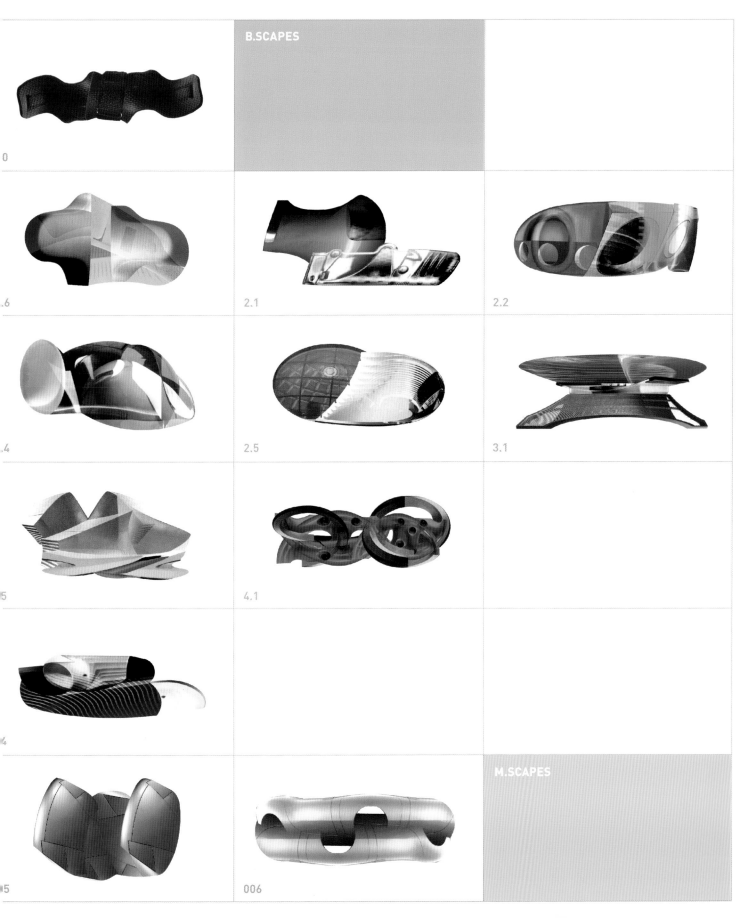

B.SCAPES

0

.6

2.1

2.2

.4

2.5

3.1

5

4.1

4

5

006

M.SCAPES

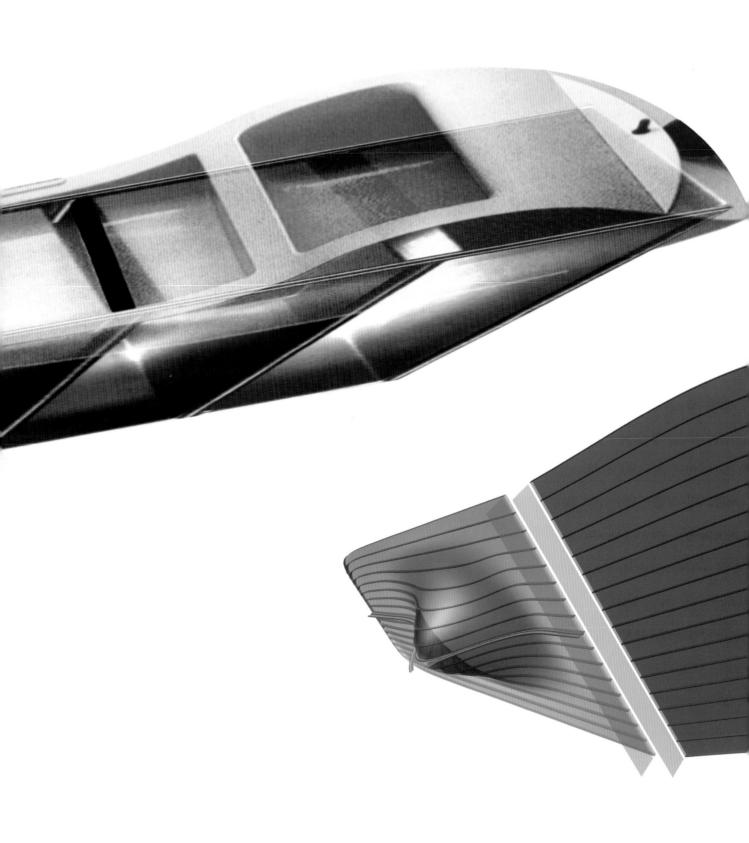

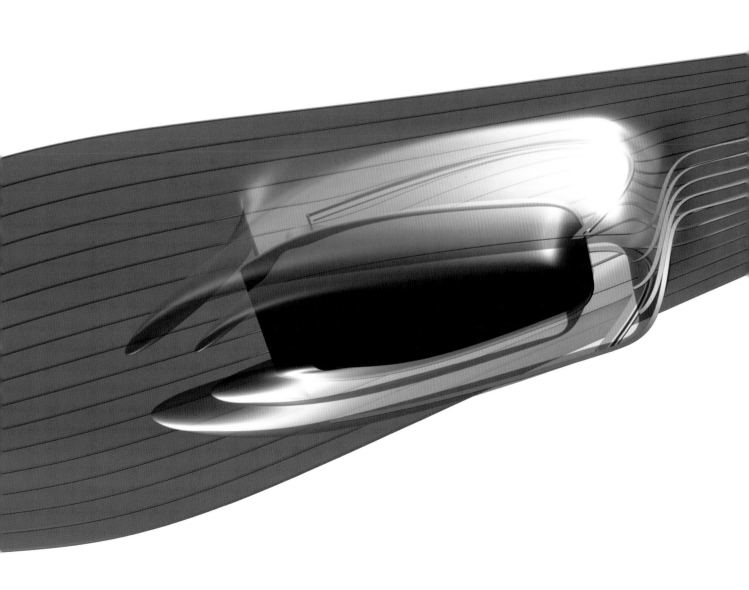

Haarlemmermeer, the area in which Schipol airport is located, is host to the Floriade 2002 World Horticultural Exhibition. The exhibition brings together nations from around the globe to present in pavilions throughout the site. Following an international competition, Asymptote was commissioned to design the main municipal pavilion, whose purpose is to promote the host city of Haarlemmermeer as a vital and growing urban environment. The Hydra-Pier pavilion houses multimedia

exhibitions and initially functions as a centerpiece of the exhibition grounds. In the future it will be used for both community-sponsored and private events.

In sharp contrast to the frequent sight overhead of airplanes from nearby Schipol airport and the endless stream of highway traffic from the surrounding urban area, the Hydra-Pier site sits nestled within a seemingly pastoral landscape. For much of the nineteenth century, the Haarlemmer-

meer region lay five meters below water. It was drained 150 years ago, and the nineteenth-century dams and pumping stations that still exist today transformed the site into habitable and usable land. The Hydra-Pier's siting on the lake marks this tenuous threshold between land and water. Water is pumped over its roof and onto the vertical surfaces of its two "water walls" in celebration of the area's rich history.

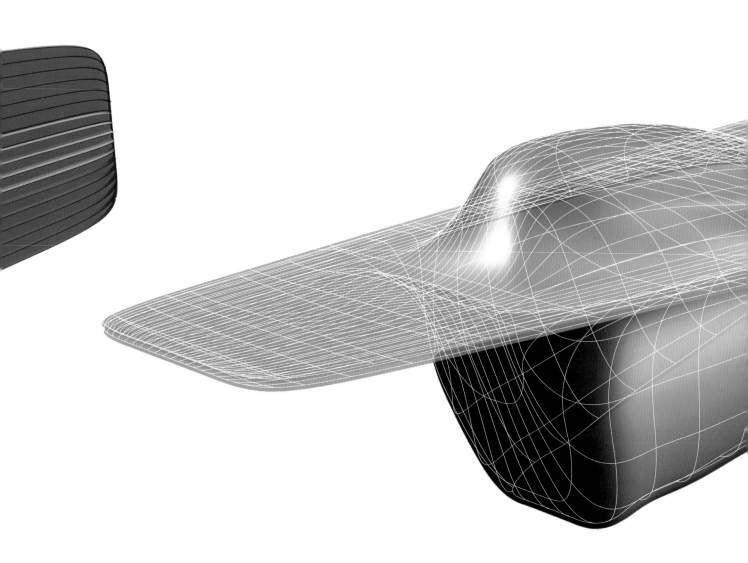

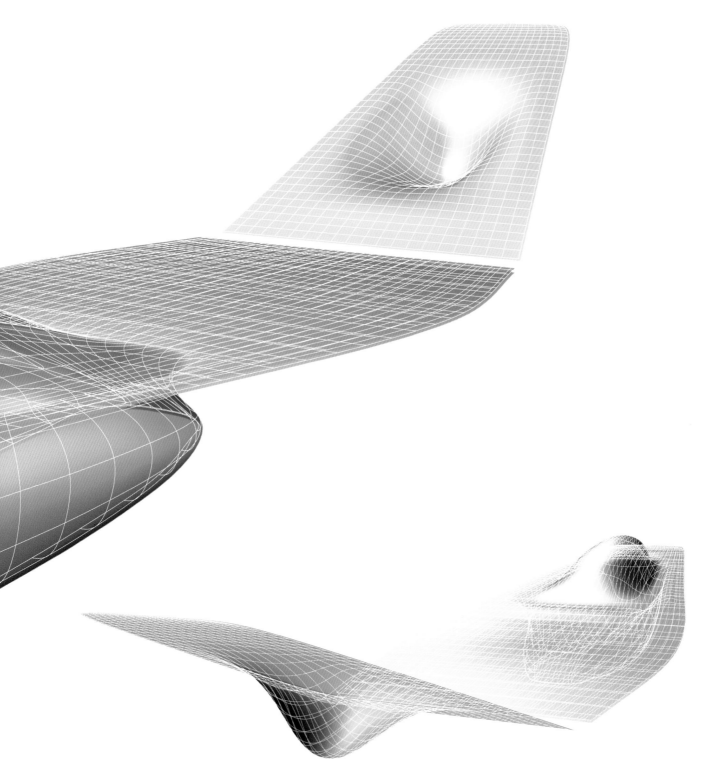

Hydra-Pier is a covered landscape on the shore of the Haarlemmermeer Bos, an entrance bridge between the two water-walls. It is also an enclosed multimedia exhibition space surrounded by a large deck that projects onto the lake. The architecture of the pavilion itself consists of two inclined, liquid-covered metallic planes deformed to incorporate an interior volume and an exterior pool. The planes become an architectural landscape that is

a combination of natural and technological forces. One enters this landscape below a glass pool that holds water at the five-meter level, marking the original water datum. Continual pumping circulates water over the aluminum surfaces, and the controlled flow of water fuses with the winglike structure to create reflective, glistening, seemingly fluid surfaces. Air travelers above or visitors at ground level will see the pavilion's uplifted, liquid, wing-

like roof reflect the sky by day, while at night they will see light and projected images emanating from it. Water is visible through the glazed underside of the pool as well as through openings in the under-side of the roof. The resultant spatial condition plays on the displacement of water relative to sea level and alludes to the artificial condition of the Hydra-Pier's natural setting.

202

1 2 3 4 5 6 7 8 9 10 11 12 13

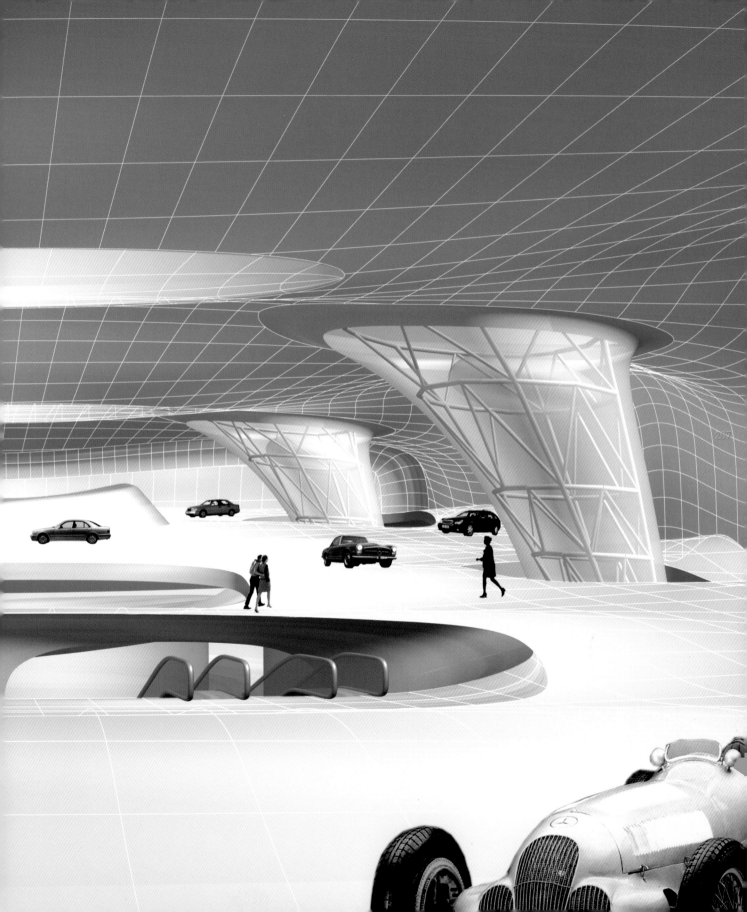

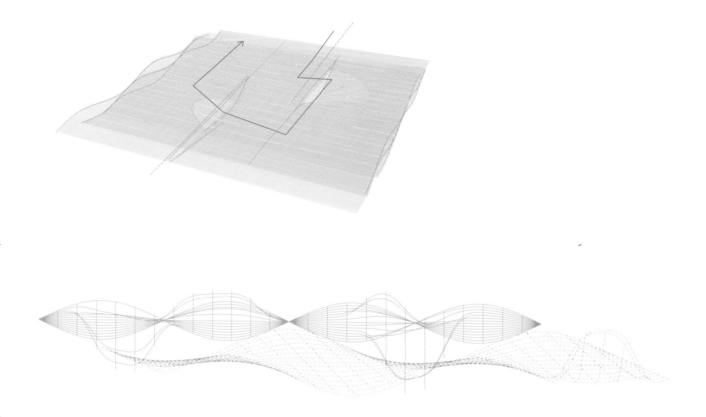

A museum for the history of the automobile as experienced through the lens of Mercedes-Benz must accommodate the rich heritage of the Mercedes brand but place it in the context of the present while looking to the future. The architecture of the museum must be original yet enduring, derived from technological precision and aesthetic sophistication that are not separate entities but completely integrated. The Mercedes Benz museum is thus based on the combined use of a large-span open space with a topologically complex surface to create a "landscape" that is both fluid and flexible. This is accomplished by applying intersecting "wave" geometries across an inclined plane spanning the entire width of the hall. The floor areas that result from this mathematical operation can accommodate an impressive collection of automobiles displayed in dynamic arrangements on various inclined and curved surfaces. The space also houses a variety of exhibition strategies for didactic material. The explanatory exhibition material can take many forms, from surface graphics to suspended video panels to transparent partitions.

Visitor paths between the display areas traverse the landscape, intersecting at various nodal points. This circulation pattern makes it possible for the visitor

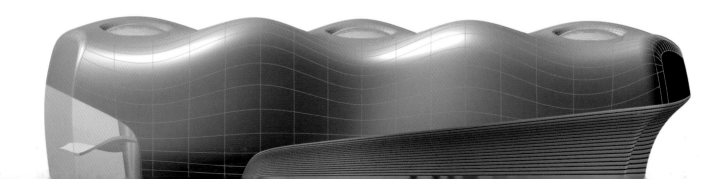

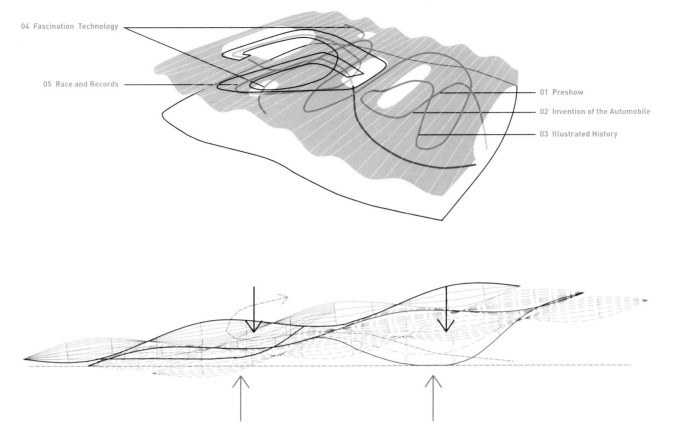

04 Fascination Technology

05 Race and Records

01 Preshow

02 Invention of the Automobile

03 Illustrated History

either to have a comprehensive experience of the whole exhibition or to pursue any number of meandering routes. At grade, the lower museum level houses the beginning and end of the exhibition tour as well as ancillary exhibition and multimedia spaces, public functions, servicing, and support areas. Openings in the upper exhibition floor create a seamless visual and physical connection to the spaces below, such as the foyer, the technology

exhibition areas, and the Racing and Records Exhibition Ramp. At the far end of the main exhibition space, at the top of the inclined floor, is a gleaming, metallic, curved volume that contains the Racing and Records Cinema. This space is open on one side and overlooks the Racing and Records ramp that descends dramatically from the upper level to the ground floor. The multistory foyer is a continuation of the museum plaza on the exterior. It is

partially open to the exhibition space above and overlooks the plaza through the broad transparent facade.

The building is enclosed by a combination of transparent, louvered, and opaque surfaces to satisfy different needs for views and daylighting. The large glazed main facade admits views into the museum from the exterior and out onto the new museum plaza from both the upper and lower level. This glass facade wraps around the main facade to provide additional visibility and access to the public programs such as the cafe, restaurant, and museum shop. On the lower levels the side and rear elevations are a double-layer facade. The building is wrapped in a metal-louvered exterior skin and an interior skin that can be either transparent, translucent, or opaque depending on the program requirements of the individual spaces. The louvered skin creates aesthetic continuity across the varied programs and provides environmental control where needed. The louvers complement the smooth, seamless glass and metal portions of the remaining building envelope. The upper elevations and the roof are clad in curved aluminum panels and glass inserts to create a smooth, taught surface not unlike that of a Mercedes-Benz car body.

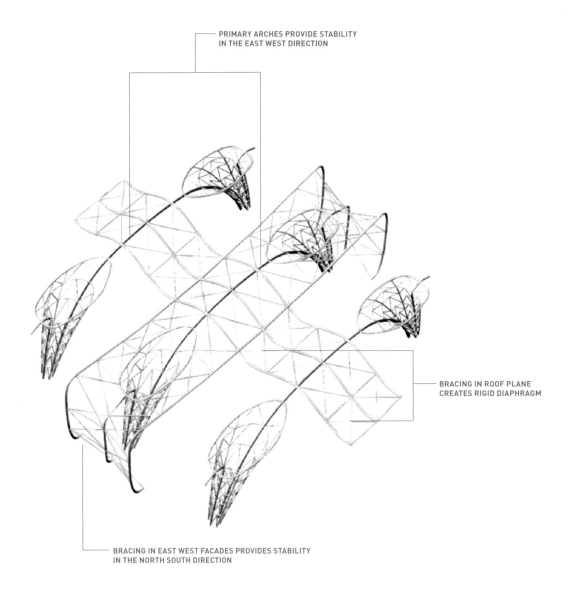

PRIMARY ARCHES PROVIDE STABILITY
IN THE EAST WEST DIRECTION

BRACING IN ROOF PLANE
CREATES RIGID DIAPHRAGM

BRACING IN EAST WEST FACADES PROVIDES STABILITY
IN THE NORTH SOUTH DIRECTION

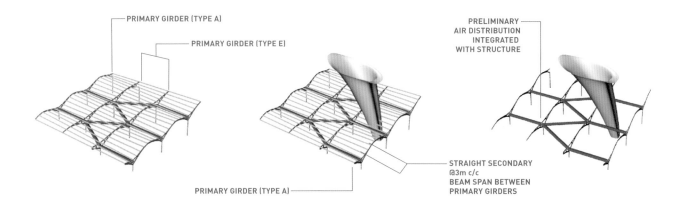

PRIMARY GIRDER (TYPE A)

PRIMARY GIRDER (TYPE E)

PRELIMINARY
AIR DISTRIBUTION
INTEGRATED
WITH STRUCTURE

PRIMARY GIRDER (TYPE A)

STRAIGHT SECONDARY
@3m c/c
BEAM SPAN BETWEEN
PRIMARY GIRDERS

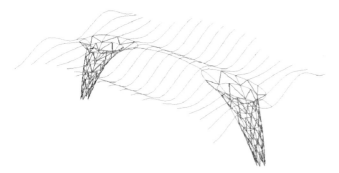

STRUCTURAL MODEL OF TYPICAL BAY

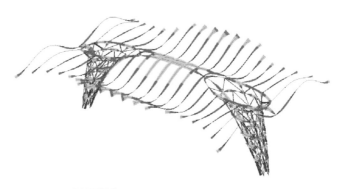

PRELIMINARY RESULTS
STRESSES UNDER DEAD AND LIVE LOAD

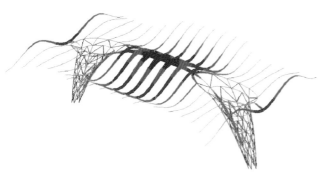

PRELIMINARY RESULTS
STRESSES UNDER DEAD AND ASYMETRIC LIVE LOAD

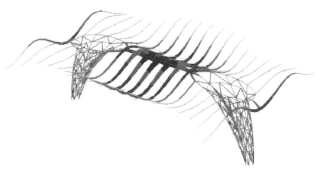

PRELIMINARY RESULTS
DEFLECTION UNDER LIVE LOAD

213

GENERAL STRUCTURE

The structure for the new exhibition hall follows closely the architectural form of the building. The intent was to merge the structure with the architecture, taking advantage of the inherent stiffness of the curving surfaces of the building to generate an efficient structural solution. The resulting structural forms tend to carry loads in the plane of the surfaces, similar to the shell structure of a car body.

The roof surface geometry is generated from parallel sine and cosine curves. A sine curve runs down both the east and west edges of the roof, with a cosine curve, of the same amplitude and wavelength, running down the middle. A similar discipline is adopted for the two floor plates, although each has a different wavelength and generator curve amplitude to suit its function. The surface created by joining these curves varies subtly across the floor and roof plates. However, the geometric discipline of the concept creates a high

degree of repetition and standardization in the components of the structure, further adding to its efficiency and economy.

A steel-framed structure is proposed. Steel can economically support the generous spans required and is an appropriate solution for the long-span exhibit hall roof.

Eyebeam Museum of Art and Technology
New York, New York

WRITING SPACE, Paper Biennale

structure

skin

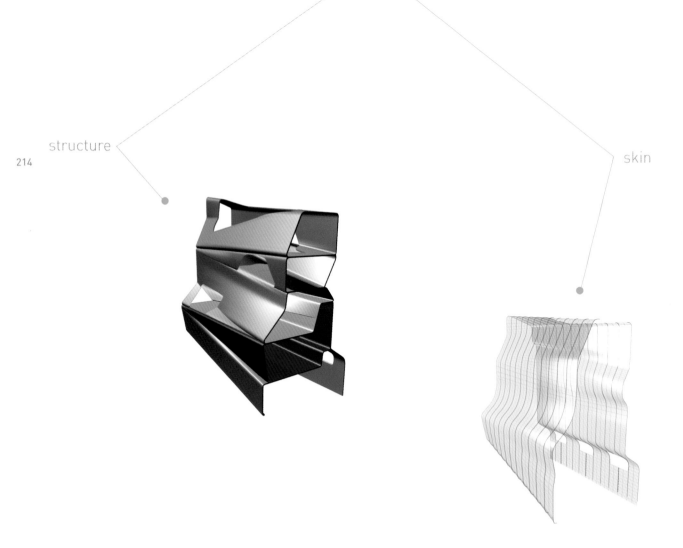

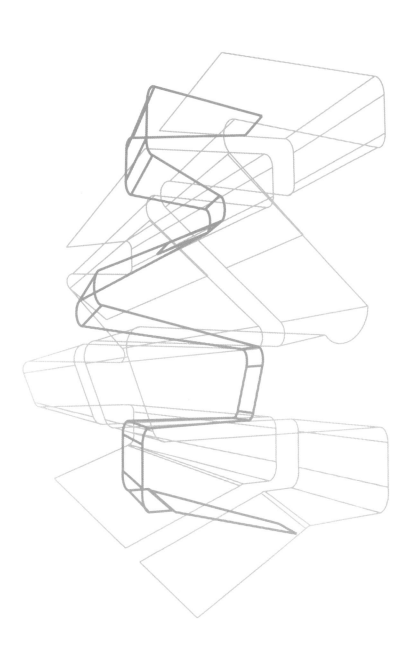

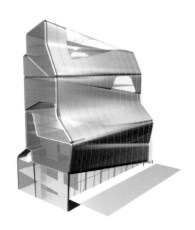

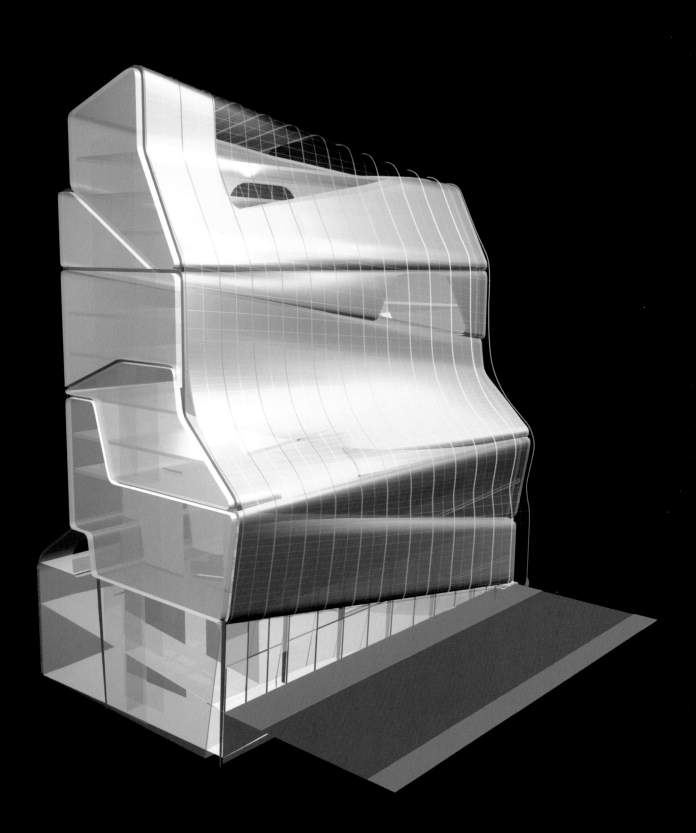

New-media art, whether it utilizes digital technology for interactive installations, video, or multimedia works, has moved the artist's mode of production and representation into entirely new arenas and assemblies. A new museum for new forms of expression must be at once a hybrid of the "traditional" museum environment and a mechanism for a fluid transfer of program and event. This new museum and atelier must mutate constantly as new forms of expression develop and occupy its interior. At the very core of the new media is the notion of flux, where narrative, image, and plasticity are elastic and ever-changing. At each moment in the building's design and formal resolution, a continual transitioning and overlapping of programs is made apparent.

EXHIBITION
The large, sloping, continuous surface at entry level creates a seamless transition to an exhibition space below grade and to a system of ramps that lead up to the public amenities, the black box theater, and the atelier programs. Above the ground-level exhibition space, a segment of the black box theater floor opens and lowers to create a new spatial connection between the two areas. This large-scale, stairlike element provides additional theater-type seating for ground-floor events. Further, it enables both spaces to accommodate a full range of overlapping and fluctuating programs, from exhibitions and events to performances and lectures. A large hydraulic lift servicing the theater is housed in the lower level of the exhibition area. As with most other components in the museum, it too has multiple functions. Beyond its service role it can be used as a stage platform, a projection booth, an exhibition vitrine, or a location for site-specific installation.

Elsewhere throughout the museum, floors and walls are equipped for data connection and multimedia display. These include a large video wall at the rear of the exhibition space, transparent projection surfaces at the cafe and bookstore, and a video pool on the floor of the lower level and along the transition ramps that meander from the main level around the theater and up through the atelier spaces.

The black box theater plays a significant role in the life of the museum. The lobby and ramps surrounding the theater and mezzanine function as transitional and transformative spaces: as an extension of the exhibition space below, of the theater space itself, and of the art education and art production areas above. As opposed to most conventional museums, where the theater or auditorium space is of secondary importance, here the theater is primary. As the digital arts continue to transform and evolve, the categories of performance and exhibition are no longer mutually exclusive. Here the theater is a space of overlap not only between exhibition and performance but between process and output. The black box theater as a new media laboratory thus becomes a valuable amenity for the art production and art education departments and provides further opportunity for interaction with the public.

The atelier as a place of experimentation, production, and education is an integral component of the museum. The atelier is linked directly with the black box theater to create a smooth transition between public museum spaces and those of the atelier. The two amenities share space for exhibitions, performances, and events. The art education and art production programs inhabit equally fluid and interrelated spatial configurations that can adapt to future transformations.

The building's skin, structural envelope, and program all result from the notions of transfer and flux. The skin is comprised of "shrink-wrapped," pixelated electronic glass capable of modulating the building transparency and conveying pattern and image to the building exterior. What is important structurally — the transfer of loads through a continuous surface — is also the conceptual basis for the program throughout the building interior. The exhibition space transforms into a theater, a loading area, and an assembly hall. The program then transfers above morphologically to a cafe, a bookstore, and to a theater with moveable floors and walls. As the walls slide away, what was once circulation becomes viewing space. The program continues to transfer and change as one moves up through the building. The ramps convert the space of display and spectacle into offices and archives, control rooms, a green room, and curator offices. The office space above is also in a state of transition from leasable offices to future gallery and atelier spaces. The roof garden itself is a transfer point between the indoor cafe and the exterior exhibit area for outdoor works. It is also a transfer point between the building and the city, where the cityscapes seemingly mutate the building's envelope.

Asymptote's B.Scape studies were presented as holographic projections at the Henry Urbach Gallery through the combination of one-way mirrored surfaces, high-resolution projection units, and computer-generated data. The gallery is situated on the tenth floor of a building in the Chelsea neighborhood of New York, which allowed the moving images to be presented in part as large-scale virtual projections over the New York skyline. The installation is an image-space initiative based on parameters of displacement and transfer, where architecture is action, space serves to control, and the body becomes a shield. The movement of the body through virtual and real space is being redefined today by information flows, image digitization, and multiple possibilities for augmentation. We inhabit this space of slippage, shuttling between plastic solidity and an ephemeral liquidity generated by light. Within these intervals are architectures of various scales with protean meanings. The body — clad, contained, and in motion — merges with the folds of mutated and transitional space, forming territories that allow us to move back and forth from virtual avatar to physical self, to be simultaneously off-side-on.

221

Claudia Hill Show
TimeSpace Installation and Fashion Show
New York, New York

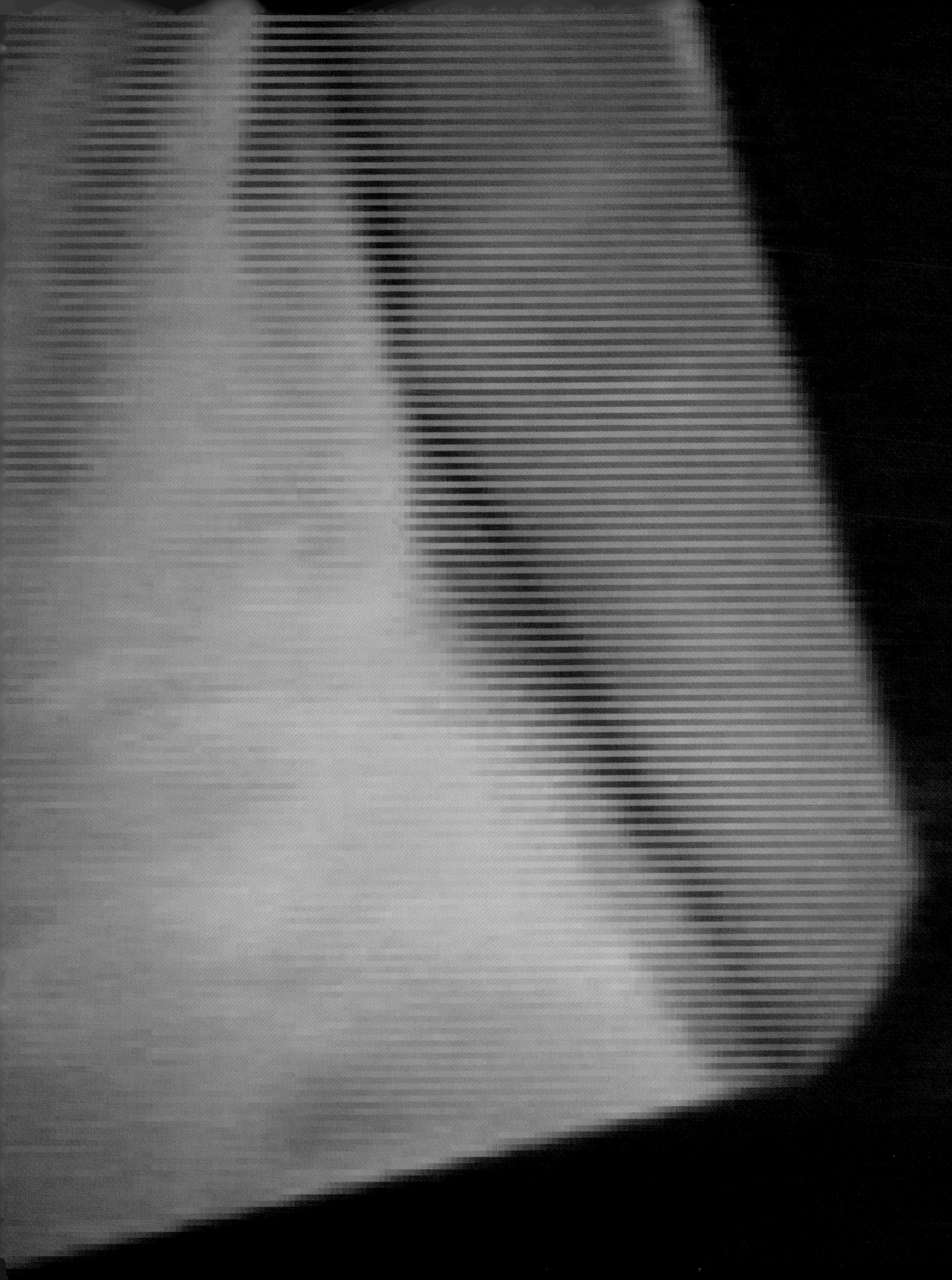

Asymptote's collaboration with fashion designer Claudia Hill afforded both creative partners the opportunity to produce a new spatial experience based on architectural mutation, temporal ambiguity, and cinematic effects. The architectural installation designed by Asymptote formed the backdrop to the fashion runway and consisted of three single-occupancy, changing-room "vitrines" interspersed with large rear-projection video screens. The changing rooms consisted of semi-transparent and semi-reflective enclosures constructed of one-way mirrors. Video cameras mounted above captured a top view of models dressing and undressing, combined with a multitude of reflections from the surrounding interior walls. A time delay was incorporated into the video images as they appeared on the large projection surfaces alongside the vitrines, where the activity was taking place in real space and real time. During the show the audience simultaneously witnessed the undressing and dressing of the models and the overlap of its own reflection on the exterior surfaces of the vitrines. In the foreground, models moved to a Butoh-like choreography and appeared to merge with the ephemeral background. The overall effect of the spatial experiment was an inversion of reality, one in which the physical presence of the audience and the actual models was doubled, replayed, augmented, and seemingly virtualized in real time and space.

Fluxspace 1.0 Installation
2000
CCAC Institute, San Francisco,
California

A multimedia installation utilizing
computer and projection technologies
in tandem with a larger-scale built
artifact equipped with touch sensors.
These "virtual buttons" are projected
onto the surface of the object and
activated by the gallery occupants.
These in turn activate a series of
video projections and soundscapes
that alter the appearance of the
artifact and create the effect of
fluctuating physical states.

h: 7 ft. w: 7 ft. l: 5 ft.
h: 2.13m w: 2.13m l: 1.52m
Multimedia video projection units,
computers, heat-sensitive receptors,
plaster, lathe, and wood

Architects
Hani Rashid and Lise Anne Couture,
Ruth Berktold, John Cleater, Noboru
Ota, Florian Pfeifer

Technical Consultant
Eric Fixler

Fluxspace 1.0 is a Capp Street Project
funded by the CCAC Institute Artist in
Residency Program.

pp. 6..11

Fluxspace 2.0 Pavilion
2000
Venice Biennale, Venice, Italy

A large-scale temporary intervention
in the historic gardens of the Venice
Biennale exposition grounds. The
two-story high, air-filled envelope
was supported by an elaborate steel-
frame structure that formed the
installation interior. Two pivoting
Plexiglas diaphragms measuring 8
feet in diameter were equipped with
IPIX cameras capable of recording
images at thirty-second intervals.
The resulting images of the constantly changing interior "architectures" were published on the Internet
in real time. The project produced
1.54 million distinct images of the
interior volume and the distortions
and changes that unfolded over the
five-month duration of the Biennale.

h: 20 ft w: 15 ft l: 40 ft
h: 6.09m w: 4.57m l: 12.19m
Pneumatic membrane and steel
structure, one-way mirrored
Plexiglas diaphragms, IPIX web
cameras, computers, fluorescent
lighting, concrete and wood foundation and flooring

Architects
Hani Rashid and Lise Anne Couture,
John Cleater, Noboru Ota, Florian
Pfeifer

Structural Engineers
Buro Happold, New York

Steel Fabrication
Metallwerkstätte,
Walter Schulz GmbH

Pneumatic Structure
Michael Schultes, Vienna

Fluxspace 2.0 was generously
supported by The Bohen Foundation.

Fluxspace 2.0 is in the collection of
the Solomon R. Guggenheim Museum.

pp. 12..21

New York Stock Exchange
Advanced Trading Floor
1997–2000
New York, New York

The main operations component
of the New York Stock Exchange's
trading floor in New York. The
Command Center houses all necessary data displays and computer
support systems as well as the
Asymptote-designed 3DTF Virtual
Reality Environment.

h: 10 ft. w: 15 ft. l: 40 ft.
h: 3.04m w: 4.57m l: 12.19m
Tempered curved glass with color
laminate, LCD flat-screen monitors,
formed steel structure, epoxy flooring, steel cabinetry, fiber optic and
cold cathode lighting

Client
New York Stock Exchange

Architects
Hani Rashid and Lise Anne Couture,
John Cleater, Elaine Didyk, Samuel
Hassler, Sabine Muller, Folker
Kleinekort, Marcos Velasques,
Kevin Estrada, Henning Meyer,
Carlos Ballestri

Lighting Design
L'Observatoir

Structural Engineers
HLW International

Contractor
Morse Diesel International

Fabrication
Milgo Bufkin Inc.

Photography
Arc Photo Eduard Hueber

pp. 22..33

NYSE 3DTF Virtual Reality
Environment
1997–2000
New York, New York

A large-scale, real-time information
model exhibiting flows and various
data-mapping capabilities for use
by the operations team at the NYSE.
The virtual-reality environment
allows users to monitor and correlate
the stock exchange's daily trading
activity and present the information
within a fully interactive, multi-
dimensional environment.

Software
Alias, Cosmo Worlds VRML, Adobe
Photoshop, Adobe Premiere

Hardware
Silicon Graphics 02 and SGI Onyx
computers

Client
New York Stock Exchange
Securities Industries Automation
Corporation, SIAC

Architects
Hani Rashid and Lise Anne Couture,
Philippe Barman, Sabine Muller,
Jan Loeken, David Serero, Tobias
Wallisser, Gemma Koppen, Suzanne
Song, Takeshi Okada, Carlos Ballestri
Remo Burkhard, Florian Baier,
Florian Pfeifer

Programmers
SIAC, Brooklyn, New York
RT-Set, Tel Aviv, Israel

Images courtesy of the New York
Stock Exchange

pp. 34..43

  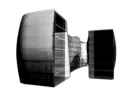

TEDX	Guggenheim Virtual Museum	BMW Event and Delivery Center	WIPO Headquarters
1999	1999–2001	2001	1998
Multi-dimensional data model	New York, New York	Munich, Germany	Geneva, Switzerland

TEDX
1999
Multi-dimensional data model

Computer-generated VRML (virtual reality markup language) artifacts that display data and statistics in multi-dimensional interactive models. These interactive data-scapes are accessible on the Internet and allow users to view data from multiple vantage points, allowing for different aspects of statistical data to be displayed and correlated.

Software
Alias, Maya, and SGI Cosmo Worlds

Architects
Hani Rashid and Lise Anne Couture, Philippe Barman, Noboru Ota, John Cleater, Peter Dorsey, David Serero, Florian Pfeifer, Lelaine Lau

Produced with the support of TED Conferences, Inc.

pp. 44..49

Guggenheim Virtual Museum
1999–2001
New York, New York

An Internet-based museum housing digital and Internet art. The Virtual Museum encompasses a number of virtual user experiences in the viewing and surveying of recent electronic acquisitions as well as other Guggenheim Museum content.

Software
Alias, Maya, Cosmo Worlds VRML, Adobe Photoshop, Adobe Premiere, Macromedia Flash

Client
Solomon R. Guggenheim Museum

Architects
Hani Rashid and Lise Anne Couture, John Cleater, Noboru Ota, David Serero, Florian Pfeifer, Ruth Ron, Birgit Schoenbrodt

Supported by The Bohen Foundation

pp. 68..79, 80

BMW Event and Delivery Center
2001
Munich, Germany

A building designed to allow visitors and customers to experience the BMW brand through a variety of functions ranging from virtual-reality simulation test-drives to showcasing the latest prototype models. The building is designed as a public facility where customers not only acquire their newly delivered automo-biles but experience the "brand" at many levels from product to spatial design. The tectonics of the building are predicated on the movement of vehicles and visitors through space. Cars are able to travel throughout the entire interior of the facility and are on show throughout their trajectory.

Client
BMW

Architects
Hani Rashid and Lise Anne Couture, Florencia Maria Pita, Ruth Berktold, Birgit Schoenbrodt, Noboru Ota, Ruth Ron, Renate Weissenboeck, Hannah Yampolsky, Alain Merkli, Moritz Schoendorf

pp. 81..87

WIPO Headquarters
1998
Geneva, Switzerland

An addition to the headquarters of the World Intellectual Property Organization, a specialized agency of the United Nations Organization.

Client
WIPO

Architects
Hani Rashid and Lise Anne Couture, Phi Barman, Ruth Berktold, Noboru Ota, Stephanie Glatz, Karen Imhoff, Ron Tannenbaum, Peter Stec

pp. 88..93

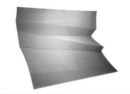

Univers Theaters
1996–1997
Aarhus, Denmark

A temporary theater structure
covering 30,000 square feet (2,787m)
of the main Bispertov square in
Aarhus. The tensile structure delin-
eates various uses and programs for
the annual Aarhus Theater Festival.
Each year new built components are
incorporated beneath the tensile
structure to facilitate the constantly
changing programs and events.

Client
Aarhus Festival

Architects
Hani Rashid and Lise Anne Couture,
Ridzwa Fathan, Oliver Neumann, Mari
Fujita, Stefan Laub, Yorick Ringeisen,
Suzanne Song, Yasmin Nicoucar,
Takeshi Okada, Bettina Zerza

Engineers
Ingenieurburo Teschner, Hamburg

Construction Management
Byggeplan data, Denmark

Photography
Torben Eskerod

pp. 94..101

Writing Space, 1996 International
Paper Biennale
1996
Hoesch Museum, Duren, Germany

Using video projection units, a
folded scrim backdrop, and digitized
sound, the installation represented
paper under various states of
manipulation and in various tectonic
conditions as an immersive multimedia installation.

h: 35 ft. w: 25 ft. d: 40 ft.
h: 10.69m w: 7.62m d: 12.19m
Theater scrim, tensile cables, video
projection and camera units,
Surround sound systems, computers

Architects
Hani Rashid and Lise Anne Couture,
Oliver Mack, Henning Meyer, Oliver
Neumann, Takeshi Okada

Awarded the second prize for the
6th International Biennale der
Papierkunst.

pp. 102..109, 214

Architexturing Copenhagen
1995
Urban design study

Computer-generated drawings
studying various locations in and
around Copenhagen. The project
incorporated experimental computer
graphic techniques into an urban
design strategy. Drawings were
developed by creating gray-scale
bump maps using imaging software
and overlaying the pattern information onto randomly selected UTM
satellite photographs. The resulting
studies yielded dimensional plans
and architectural artifacts as proposals for various locations within
the city.

Architects
Hani Rashid and Lise Anne Couture,
Kevin Estrada, Ridzwa Fathan, Yair
Millet, Lynne Miyamoto

Initially exhibited in December 1995
in the "Overlooking Copenhagen"
exhibition at the Charlottenborg in
Copenhagen.

pp. 110..114

Experimental Music Theater
1998
Graz, Austria

A new theater for the performance
of various music events and genres.
The building itself is an adjustable
apparatus allowing for differing
configurations and acoustic possibilities, thereby affording composers and
performers the opportunity to tailor
the building to their specific musical
requirements. The building is also
capable of being used as a "sound
box" acoustically augmenting the
performance within and enhancing
the sounds as they filter into the city
space surrounding the structure.

Client
University of Graz

Architects
Hani Rashid and Lise Anne Couture,
David Serero, Kevin Estrada, Florian
Baier, Folker Kleinekort

pp. 115..119

Technology Culture Museum
1999
New York, New York

A proposal for a museum situated along the East River in lower Manhattan. The project is based on a hybrid of sports stadia and the building typology of convention centers and other large-scale display and exposition halls. Together these combined building types allow for a highly versatile, technological building that affords the opportunity to display a vast array of objects and artifacts of various spatial configurations and types.

Architects
Hani Rashid and Lise Anne Couture, Noboru Ota, John Cleater, David Serero, Florian Pfieffer

Project commissioned and supported by *Architectural Record*/"Millennium" special issue, December 1999.

pp. 122..125

Kyoto Mutimedia Center
1996–1998
Kyoto, Japan

Design for a small facility for the Kyoto Research Park consisting of television studios, loft-type work spaces for IT development, a technology museum, and multimedia theater. The project was developed as part of an initiative by Osaka Gas to build a self-contained multimedia research center and an accompanying public showcase.

Client
Osaka Gas; Kyoto Research Park, Kyoto Japan

Architects
Hani Rashid and Lise Anne Couture, John Cleater, Elaine Didyk, David Serero, Folker Kleinekort

pp. 126..129

Kyoto Research Park
1996–1998
Kyoto, Japan

A large-scale development project consisting of retail facilities, a hotel, health club, office space, restaurants, and theaters. The project is a public face for Osaka Gas, presenting various public amenities and functions along the urban edge of the site. The facilities are all designed as technological showcases that allow visitors and users to interface with the buildings through a mix of urban design and technology.

Client
Osaka Gas, Kyoto Research Park, Kyoto Japan

Architects
Hani Rashid and Lise Anne Couture, Ridzwa Fathan, John Cleater, Sabine Muller, David Serero, Folker Kleinekort, Mina Hatano, Diogo S. Lopez, Paolo Lopez, Oliver Mack, Takeshi Okada

pp. 130..131

B.Scapes
1999
Drawing and imaging studies

Computer-generated studies of the movement and tectonics of the body as a dynamic condition. The B.Scapes utilized sports gear and equipment in mapping the body's interstitial space between stasis and movement. The B.Scapes were animated in 3-D and film software to create fully dimensional artifacts for research and exhibition purposes.

24" x 36" (60.96 x 91.44 cm) Iris prints and video-generated morphs

Architects
Hani Rashid and Lise Anne Couture, David Serero, Sabine Muller, Suzanne Song

B.Scapes were first exhibited at Henry Urbach Gallery, New York, in the intallation OffsideOn in 1999. The B.Scapes were also shown in "Compression," a group show at the Feigen Gallery, New York, in 2001, and in "Vision and Reality," an exhibition at the Louisiana Museum of Modern Art in Copenhagen, also in 2001.

pp. 88..89, 132..139, 19..195

Knoll A3 Furniture System
1999–2002

The Knoll A3 system remedies many
of the problems we associate with
cubicle environments while accommodating new modes of working and
interacting in the office. Some of the
issues addressed include: new sense
of privacy without rigid opaque enclosure, sound attenuation, new forms of
cable management in which access
and reconfigurability are quicker and
more effective, workstations that can
be reconfigured easily and tailored to
the specific needs of fast-growing and
changing companies. The A3 offers
customized skins and new color
palettes to allow personalization and
fresh new aesthetics as well as ease
of ordering, manufacturing, and
shipping, with a tie-in to the Internet.
The system consists of bent steel
tubing, MDF, form-injected molded
ABS plastics, Knoll A3 fabrics, and
die-cast zinc.

Client
Knoll, New York

Architects
Hani Rashid and Lise Anne Couture,
Noboru Ota, Jose Salinas, Birgit
Schoenbrodt, Renate Weissenboeck,
Hannah Yampolsky

Knoll Team
Karen Stone, Director of Design,
Douglas Reuter, Director
of Marketing

Engineer
Knoll Product Development, East
Greenville Pennsylvania

Fabrication Consultants
Tip Sempler, Bill Shea

Photography
Ramak Fazel

pp. 140..149

A3 Showroom
2001
Chicago, Illinois

The A3 showroom design for Knoll,
Chicago during NeoCon 2000, the
annual trade show for facilities
management and interior design.
This minimal and digitally enhanced
showcase for the A3 product line used
Barrisol ceilings, holographic light-
projection boxes, flat-screen video
monitors, and lenticular imaging
panels.

Client
Knoll, New York

Architects
Hani Rashid and Lise Anne Couture,
Ruth Berktold, John Cleater, Hannah
Yampolsky

Planning Consultant
Karen Stone

Associate Architect
De Stefano & Partners, Chicago

Multimedia Consultants
Scharf Weisburg, New York

pp. 150..151

Guggenheim Center for Art
and Technology
1999–2000
New York, New York

Renovation of the SoHo Guggenheim
Museum ground floor space for the
Guggenheim Center for Art and
Technology incorporates a number
of transformable "vitrines" for showcasing design objects. It also contains
large flat-screen LCD monitors for
viewing information, ordering product
and viewing digital art content. The
intervention creates a space between
Broadway and Prince streets and
bridges the new Guggenheim space
with the Soho Prada store.

Client
Solomon R. Guggenheim Museum

Architects
Hani Rashid and Lise Anne Couture,
John Cleater, Elaine Didyk, Ruth
Berktold, David Serero, Florian
Pfieffer, Ole Smith, Florencia Maria
Pita, Moritz Schondorf, Sven Steiner

Photography courtesy of David Heald,
Solomon R. Guggenheim Foundation
photo department.

pp. 152..157

Airport Urbanism
2000
Project

This project explored airports as
surrogate urban centers that provide
many of the amenities, events, and
attributes of the cities which they are
tethered to and reliant on. The future
of city space is implicitly tied to air
travel and airport infrastructure. The
notion of the central business district
as a place relegated solely to city
centers is now becoming obsolete.
Instead, new city space is beginning
to prevail at airports, and to be
dislodged from any one place and
strewn throughout the globe. Airport
Urbanism is a study of such a phenomenon, where the future of both
airports and cities is fused as a singular initiative. This new city space is
where business meetings, health
clubs, recreational facilities, and even
housing are all developed within the
space of what we traditionally called
the airport.

Architects
Hani Rashid and Lise Anne Couture,
Herman Zschiegner, Birgit
Schoenbrodt

pp. 158..165

Dodger Stadium
2000
Los Angeles, California

A new baseball stadium proposal for the Los Angeles Dodgers to be built on the existing stadium site in Los Angeles. The new building has a completely climate-controlled playing field and bleachers covered by a pneumatic dome structure. The inflatable roof is capable of producing colored patterns that are electronically controlled. The changing color and density of the pneumatic membranes allow graphics, logos, and other streaming information to be "broadcast" on the roof for aerial and internal viewing.

Architects
Hani Rashid and Lise Anne Couture,
John Cleater, Noboru Ota

pp. 166..169

The Incubator
1999
Armory Building, San Francisco, California

In order to accommodate burgeoning multimedia and e-commerce ventures, the existing Armory Building in San Francisco's Mission District was selected as a development site. The building contains one of the largest open-span interior spaces in the United States. The building proposal called for inserting within the existing interior a new seven-story-high, free-standing structure. An egg-shaped freestanding structure maximizes the occupiable volume to create 270,000 square feet (25,000 square meters) of rentable office space with additional public amenities including basketball courts, a swimming pool, a library, and a restaurant on the lower level. Located at the core of the scheme is a light trap, a void in the center of the building that draws light from a large skylight down through the building interior using fresnel lens technology.

Client
Ekon Investments, Houston

Architects
Hani Rashid and Lise Anne Couture,
Ruth Berktold, Noboru Ota,
Ruth Ron, Birgit Schoenbrodt,
Renate Weissenboeck

Associate Architect
Gensler, San Francisco, California

Engineer
Murphy Burr Curry, Inc.,
San Francisco

Contractor
Swinerton & Walberg Builders
San Francisco, California

pp. 170..173

I.Scapes
1999
Digital drawings

The proliferation of images prompted this series of works. Each I.Scape is a manipulated entity using a combination of image collage, three-dimensional models, and texture maps to create ambiguous images and territories that can be read as object and field simultaneously.

18" x 24" (45.72 x 60.96 cm)
Iris prints

I.Scapes 1.0 were first exhibited at Frederieke Taylor–TZ Art Gallery in New York during the exhibition of the same name. The drawings were subsequently shown at the Julie Saul Gallery in New York, in 2000, and The Brooklyn Museum in 2001

Architects
Hani Rashid and Lise Anne Couture

pp. 8, 12, 169, **174..181**, 194..196

I.Scape Multiple
1999
Frederieke Taylor–TZ Art Gallery,
New York, New York

h: 18" w: 18" d: 18"
h: 45.72cm w: 45.72cm d: 45.72cm
Sony DV players, Plexiglas "vitrines,"
Adicom infrared timing sensors

The I.scape Multiple is a digital image/model contained in a small vitrine and set to be activated perpetually, displaying the I.Scape studies as they were originally conceived in movement.

The I.Scape Multiple is part of the following museum collections:

San Francisco Museum of Modern Art
(SFMOMA)
Canadian Center for Architecture,
Montreal
Netherlands Institute for Architecture
(NAI), Rotterdam
The Solomon R. Guggenheim Museum
The Museum of Modern Art, New York

Architects
Hani Rashid and Lise Anne Couture,
John Cleater, Kevin Estrada, David
Serero, Katrin Kalden

Photography
Paul Warchol

pp. 182..183

I.Scapes Installation
1999
Frederieke Taylor–TZ Art Gallery,
New York, New York

The installation incorporated the I.Scapes studies into morphing assemblies that were transmitted onto 24 flat-screen LCD monitors. The monitors were set into a free-standing structure constructed of one-way Plexiglas sheets that reflected and refracted the moving images within the structure's interior. The images were in constant motion produced by means of morphing software and were transmitted into the installation's interior .

h: 8 ft. w: 8 ft. l:15 ft.
h: 2.44m w: 2.44m l: 4.57m
One-way mirrored Plexiglas, auto poles, Pixel-Vision LCD monitors, computers

Architects
Hani Rashid and Lise Anne Couture, John Cleater, David Serero, Kevin Estrada, Katrin Kalden, Remo Burkhard

Technical consultant
Pixel-Vision, Mike Odryna

Photography
Paul Warchol

Supported in part by Pixel-Vision Inc. USA

pp. 184..187

M.Scapes
2001
Digital drawings

Computer-generated studies of the tectonics of movement manifest through automotive styling and modeling. The M.Scapes were produced with modeling software to create new assemblies that addressed the formal aesthetics of movement and speed reinterpreted as static artifacts.

30" x 40" (76.2 x 101.6 cm) Iris prints

M.Scapes were first exhibited at the Institute for Contemporary Art (ICA) in Philadelphia in December 2000 as part of the Stratascape installation.

Architects
Hani Rashid and Lise Anne Couture

pp. 188..193, 194..195

Hydra-Pier
2001
Haarlemmermeer,
The Netherlands

The Hydra-Pier is the main gateway pavilion for the Floriade festival in Haarlemmermeer. The project is sited near Shipol Airport and commemorates both the technologies of flight and of land retrieval through the pumping of vast quantities of water. The structure is 100 meters (300 feet) long and sited on an artificial body of water and landscape. When activated, the pavilion is covered in a sheath of water that cascades over its entire envelope, forming two vertical planes of water through which people enter.

Client
Municipality of Haarlemmermeer

Architects
Hani Rashid and Lise Anne Couture, Elaine Didyk, Birgit Schoenbrodt, Jose Salinas, John Cleater, Martin Thue Jacobsen, Alain Merkli, Moritz Schoendorf, Rafal Bajuk

Associate Architect
Architektenburo Bronsvoort bna. Anton Bronsvoort, principal

Structural Engineers
Ingenieursburo, Smit Westerman

Glass Structure
Octatube, bv.

Water Engineering
Lotek

Contractor
Nijhuis Bouw bv., Utrecht

Project management
Infocus Bouwmanagement bv.

Lighting Consultant
Hollands Licht

Special acknowledgement for the support of Niek Verdonk

pp. 196..205

Mercedes-Benz Museum of the Automobile
2001
Stuttgart, Germany

The museum is designed to house the impressive collection of automobiles and associated content pertaining to Mercedes-Benz and their legacy. The main exhibition hall displays the entire history of Mercedes Benz automobiles on an undulating topological surface This tectonic interior "landscape" provides numerous modes of display and viewing for visitors and curators. The building roof, floor, and cladding systems are integrated utilizing technologies and tectonics that are already part of automotive manufacture and design. At the terminus of the building's grand interior, a race track displays speed-record-setting cars.

Client
Daimler Chrysler, Stuttgart, Germany

Architects
Hani Rashid and Lise Anne Couture, Ruth Berktold, Jose Salinas, Birgit Schoenbrodt, John Cleater, Noboru Ota, Hannah Yampolsky, Jonas Brasse, Andreas Derkum, Cathrin Loose, Markus Randler

Engineers
Ove Arup, New York

pp. 206..213

Eyebeam Museum of Art
and Technology
2001
New York, New York

A proposal for a new museum for
digital art in the Chelsea district of
Manhattan. The proposal consisted of
an inner-block insertion that provides
exhibition, delivery, auditorium, and
event spaces on the street level and
various gallery spaces and offices on
the upper floors. The project was
developed with the idea of maximiz-
ing the galleries' usability and acces-
sibility through "hinging" floors and
transformable interior spaces. The
structure is comprised of folded
pre-stressed concrete slabs and is
column free. The exterior skin is
made up of electronically infused
glass panels capable of displaying
256 shades of gray. Through computer programming it can display
large-scale moving images over the
entire building skin.

Client
Eyebeam Atelier/John Johnson

Architects
Hani Rashid and Lise Anne Couture,
Ruth Berktold, John Cleater, Jose
Salinas, Noboru Ota, Birgit
Schoenbrodt, Renate Weissenboeck,
Hannah Yampolsky, Alain Merkli,
Moritz Schoendorf

pp. 214..219

OffsideOn Installation
1999
Henry Urbach Gallery, New York,
New York

Through the combination of one-way
mirrored surfaces, high-resolution
projection units, and computer-
generated data, the B.Scape studies
were presented as holographic projections into the space of the gallery.
Henry Urbach Gallery is situated on
the tenth floor of a Chelsea building
in New York. This approach to exhibiting the B.Scapes allowed the moving
images to be presented as large-
scale virtual projections over the New
York skyline while viewed from within
the gallery installation.

h: 8 ft. w: 8 ft. d: 12 ft.
h: 2.44m w: 2.44m d: 3.66m
Plexiglas, auto poles,
video projection units, computers

Architects
Hani Rashid and Lise Anne Couture,
John Cleater, David Serero, Kevin
Estrada, Remo Burkhard, Sabine
Muller, Suzanne Song, Jennifer Fern

pp. 220..221

Claudia Hill Show
2000
Eyebeam Atelier, New York, New York

A collaborative project with the
fashion designer Claudia Hill took
place in the Eyebeam Atelier in New
York. The project consisted of three
one-way mirrored-glass vitrines set
on a stage and used by the models
during the performance. The vitrines
were equipped with Web cams that
broadcast "digitally abstract" movement of the body onto large screens
adjacent to the vitrines. The choreography of slow movement by Hill was
designed to contrast with the fast
movement caught by the cameras and
projected in real time as large-
format video images.

Architects
Hani Rashid and Lise Anne Couture,
Ruth Berktold, John Cleater

pp. 221, 222..227

Asymptote Flux
2002
New York, New York

Asymptote Flux is a survey of works
by Hani Rashid and Lise Anne Couture
that eschews conventional methods
of presentation through chronology or
project type and instead makes transparent the affiliations and connective
strategies that surface continually
throughout their oeuvre. The book
invokes a set of ideas that are constantly evolving and transforming
irrespective of scale, category, or
medium. Special thanks to the following individuals who are true believers
in the asymptotic trajectory: Allan
Chasanoff, Thomas Krens, Judith Cox,
Mathew Drutt, Fred Henry, Max
Hollein, Andrew Cogan, Aaron Betsky,
Thomas Leeser, Frederic Migayrou,
Dror Segal, Kristin Feiress, Zaha
Hadid, Massimiliano Fuksas,
Frederieke Taylor, Henry Urbach,
Claudia Gould, Karim Rashid, Luca
Molinari, Richard Castelli, Lars
Seeberg, Niek Verdonk, Wiel Arets,
Bernard Tschumi, Okwui Enwezor.

210mm x 245mm, 240 pages

Designer
Hannah Yampolsky, Asymptote

Writing Contributions:
Virtual Architecture — Real Space
by Hani Rashid and Lise Anne Couture
pp. 50..51

Investigations
by Hani Rashid
pp. 52..55

Christian Pongratz and Maria-Rita
Perbellini Interview Hani Rashid
pp. 56..58

Federico Chiara Interviews Asymptote
for Italian *Vogue*
pp. 59..62

Putri Trisulo Interviews Hani Rashid
for *Transmission*
pp. 63..65

Installing Space
by Hani Rashid
pp. 66..67

SELECTED PROJECTS

2001   Mercedes-Benz Museum of the Automobile–competition, Stuttgart, Germany
         BMW Event and Delivery Center–competition, Munich, Germany
         Eyebeam Museum of Art and Technology (FluxMuseum)–competition, New York, USA
         Hydra-Pier–competition (1st Prize), Harlemmermeer, The Netherlands
         Knoll Showroom, Chicago, USA
         Knoll A3 Furniture System, New York, USA
         Queen's Museum Expansion–competition, New York, USA

2000   The Incubator, San Francisco, USA
         King Street Residences, San Francisco, USA
         Guggenheim Offices, New York, USA
         WIPO Headquarters–competition, Geneva, Switzerland
         Beukenhorst Masterplan–competition (1st Prize), Amsterdam, The Netherlands
         Graduate School of Fine Arts, Columbia University, New York, USA
         NYSE 3DTF Virtual Reality Environment, New York, USA
         Issey Miyake Flagship Store, New York, USA

1999   Guggenheim Center for Art and Technology, New York, USA
         NYSE Advanced Trading Floor, New York, USA
         Guggenheim Virtual Museum, New York, USA
         Artist's Residence, New York, USA
         Stream House, Connecticut, USA

1998   Kyoto Multimedia Center, Kyoto, Japan
         Experimental Music Theater–competition, Graz, Austria
         New York Stock Exchange 3DTF Virtual Reality Environment, Phase 2, New York, USA

1997   LegoZone Display Area, Billund, Denmark
         Aarhus Museum of Modern Art–competition, Aarhus, Denmark
         New York Stock Exchange 3DTF Virtual Reality Environment, Phase 1, New York, USA

1996   Univers Multimedia Theater, Aarhus, Denmark
         Universal City Osaka Masterplan, Osaka, Japan
         Kyoto Multimedia Center, Kyoto, Japan

1995   National Gallery of Korea–competition (selected for the Korean Pavilion, Seoul, South Korea, 1998)

1994   International Seaport Terminal–competition, Yokohama, Japan
         Tohoku Historical Museum–competition, Sendai, Japan

1993   Contemporary Arts Center–competition (4th Place), Tours, France
         Mariko Transport Co. Headquarters, Tokyo, Japan

1992   Times Square Interventions, New York, USA
         Parliamentary Precinct / Spreebogen–competition, Berlin, Germany

1991   National Dutch Courthouse–competition (1st Place), Groningen, The Netherlands
         Housing and Masterplan–competition, Munich, Germany
         Six Housing Units, Brig, Switzerland
         "Light Prop" Public Art Project, Toronto, Canada

1990   Moscow State Theater–competition (Honorable Mention), Moscow, Russia

1989   Library of Alexandria–competition (4th Place), Alexandria, Egypt

1988   West Coast Gateway (Steel Cloud)–competition (1st Place), Los Angeles, USA

EXHIBITIONS

2002   Design Exchange, Toronto, Ontario, "New Landscape: Design Transforms Canadian Furniture"
         Max Protetch Gallery, New York, USA, "A New World Trade Center: Design Proposals"

2001   ICA, Philadelphia, Pennsylvania, "Stratascape"
         Eyebeam Atelier, New York, USA, "Open Source Architecture: Building Eyebeam"
         Deutsches Architektur Museum, Frankfurt, Germany, "Digital/Real"
         San Francisco Museum of Modern Art, USA, "010101"
         Kunstlerhaus, Vienna, Austria, "Global Tools"
         Brooklyn Museum of Art, Brooklyn, New York, USA, "Digital Printmaking Now"
         Davison Art Center, Middletown, Connecticut, USA, "Abstraction and Representation"

2000	Julie Saul Gallery, New York, USA, "Architectural Constructs"
	California College of Arts and Crafts (CCAC), San Francisco, USA, "Fluxspace 1.0"
	Venice Biennale of Architecture, Venice, Italy, "Fluxspace 2.0"
	Louisiana Museum, Copenhagen, Denmark, "Vision and Reality"
	CVAC, Storrs, Connecticut, USA, "WorkingDigital"
	Galerie Cato Jans, Hamburg, Germany, "Millenium Futures to Come"
	Feigen Gallery, New York, USA, "Compressions"
1999	Frederieke Taylor–TZ Art Gallery, New York, USA, "(un) comfortable surroundings"
	Museum of Modern Art, New York, USA, Selections from the Permanant Collection
	University Art Museum, Berkeley, California, USA, "Equal Partners"
	FRAC, Orléans, France, "Archilab"
	Henry Urbach Architecture, New York, USA, "OffsideOn"
	Frederieke Taylor–TZ Art Gallery, New York, USA, "I.Scapes v. 1.0"
	Synworld, Vienna, Austria, "playwork: hyperspace"
	German Architecture Center-DAZ, Berlin, Germany, "Space '99"
	Numark Gallery, Washington, D.C., USA, "Digital Sites"
	Parsons School of Design, New York, USA, "architecture at the edge"
	Canadian Center for Architecture, Montreal, Canada, "Enchantier: Collections of the CCA"
	Dansk Arkitektur / Gammeldok, Copenhagen, Denmark, "Mutations"
	Max Protech, New York, USA, "Millenium Futures to Come"
	Julie Saul Gallery, New York, USA, "Digital Sites" Group Show
1998	Smith College Museum of Art, Northampton, Massachusetts, USA, "Equal Partners"
	American Academy in Rome, Rome, Italy, "@Edge"
	Aedes Galerie, Berlin, Germany, "TransArchitectures"
	Parsons School of Design, New York, USA, "Declassified"
1997	Musée de Montagris, Montagris, France, "Points de Vue"
	Radhushallen, Aarhus, Denmark, "Aarhus Kunstmuseum"
	Kunsthalle, Vienna, Austria, "Artistes/Architects"
	Hoesch-Museum, Duren, Germany, "International Paper Art Biennale"
1996	Venice Biennale of Architecture, Korean Pavilion, "Future Visions for Korea"
	Belem Cultural Center, Lisbon, Portugal, "Artistes/Architects"
	TZ Art Gallery, New York, USA, "Bare Bones"
	Kuntsverein, Munich, Germany, "Artistes/Architects"
	Charlottenborg, Copenhagen, Denmark, "Overlooking the City"
	Nouveau Musée, Villeurbanne, France, "Artistes/Architects"
1994	Canadian Center for Architecture, Montreal, Canada, "Urban Revisions"
	Takashimaya Gallery, Kyoto, Japan, "Future City Art Museum"
	Uzzan Galerie, Paris, France, "Hyperfine Splitting"
	Museum of Contemporary Art, Los Angeles, USA, "Urban Revisions"
	Contemporary Cultural Center, Tours, France, "L'architecte est sur les lieux"
	Musée des Beaux Arts, Chartres, France, "L'architecte est sur les lieux"
1993	German Cultural Center, New York, USA, "Designing a Capital"
	Columbia University, New York, USA, "Berlin Spreebogen"
	Whiteleys, London, England, "Theory & Experimentation"
1991	Sadock & Uzzan Galerie, Paris, France, "Les Architectes Plasticiens"
1990	Princeton University, Princeton, USA, "Anaglyptic Architecture"
	Buell Hall, New York, USA, "Optigraph 3"
	Fenster Gallery, Frankfurt, Germany, "Asymptote"
	Unesco Headquarters Gallery, Paris, France, "Alexandria Library Competition"
	Kunsthalle, Berlin, Germany, "Paris–Architektur und Utopie"
1989	Aedes Galerie, Berlin, Germany, "Experimental Architecture"
	Pacific Design Center, Los Angeles, USA, "West Coast Gateway"
	Emily Carr Gallery 76, Vancouver, Canada, "Asymptote–Selected Projects"
	AEDES/Pavilion de l'Arsenal, Paris, France, "Paris–21st Century"
	Gallery 76, Toronto, Canada, "Asymptote–Selected Projects"
	Steelcase Gallery, New York, USA, "30 Under 30"
	Griffiths McGear Gallery, New York, USA, "Form; Being; Absence"
1988	Artists Space, New York, USA, "Kursaal for an Evacuee"

PUBLICATIONS

2001

Architettura OFX — "Asymptote Architecture," by Pierantonio Giacoppo and Jamie Schwartz (Nov.-Dec., No. 63), Italy, pp. 128–35.

Report On Business — "Well Rounded," by Maryam Sanati (December), Toronto, pp. 22–23.

Metropolis — "The Rashid Machine," by Peter Hall (February), New York, pp. 42–49; 77–79.

Futur(e)s — "A Quoi Revent Les Architectes," by Isabelle Barre and Donatien Garnier (April), Paris, pp. 82–87.

Summa + — "Mentiras Ver Daderas," by Florencia Rodriguez and Gonzalo Casals (Dec., No. 52), pp. 58–61.

Architectural Review — "Reflections on the Virtual in Architecture," by Leon van Schaik (No. 74), Melbourne, Australia, pp. 42–47.

010101: Art in Technological Times — "Asymptote." Catalogue by Aaron Betsky (San Francisco: San Francisco Museum of Modern Art), pp. 30–31.

Architecture — "Asymptote Takes the Cube Out of the Cubicle," by Paul A. Barreneche (July), pp. 94–101.

Archilab — "Asymptote." Book edited by Frédéric Migayrou and Marie-Ange Brayer (Orléans, France: FRAC Centre), pp. 50–58.

The Architect — "Lise Anne Couture." Book edited by Maggie Toy (New York: Watson-Guptill), pp. 36–41.

Zoo — "Asymptote Architecture: Floriade," edited by Elisa Williams (Issue 9), UK, p. 254.

Digital / Real: Blobmeister — "Theatre of Operations for the 21st Century." Catalogue edited by Peter Cachola Schmal (Basel: Birkhauser), pp. 82–89.

Cyberspace — "Asymptote Architecture: Guggenheim Virtual Museum." Australia, pp. 84–89.

The Art of Architecture Exhibitions — "Installing space," by Kristin Feireiss and Hani Rashid (Rotterdam: NAi Publishers), pp. 34–41.

Anything — "Architecture as Interface," by Hani Rashid. ANY Conference series (Cambridge, Mass.: The MIT Press), pp. 49–54.

Dialogue — "Digital Architeture: Guggenheim's Virtual Museum Cyberspace" (Feb.), Taiwan, pp. 86–93.

Architectural Design — "Young Blood: US Pavillion, Venice Biennale 2000," by Hani Rashid (Feb.), London, pp. 84–87.

Frame: Virtual Interiors Annual 2001 — "Morph Thing," by Jan-Willem Poels (Amsterdam: Vivid Design Gallery), pp. 12–29.

Atlas — "Interior Expansion of the NYSE." Book by Luca Molinari (Paris: Skira/Seuil), pp. 129–37.

Van Alen Report — "Asymptote Public Profile," by Zoe Ryan (Dec.), Van Alen Institute, New York, pp. 26–27.

Skylines (Austrian Airlines) — "Sportdomes," by Vagn Sorensen (No. 6), p. 28.

The New York Times — "As Work and Life Blur, Office Furniture Goes 24/7," by Alastair Gordon (Sept. 2, 2001, Money and Business section).

Zlaty Rez — "Redefining Architecture: How Virtual Spaces Change Real Places," by Hani Rashid (Vol. 22), Czech Republic, pp. 36–4[?]

2000

Natural Born CAADesigners — Book by Christian Pongratz and Maria Perbellini (Basel: Birkhauser), pp. 71–84.

Abitare A — "Venezia. Architettura. Biennale," by Maria Zunino (July/August), Italy, pp. 52–71.

Ec/Arts — "The Technology Culture Museum New York," edited by Eric Sabine (issue #2), France, pp. 6-7, 64–71.

Wired — "Reinventing the Museum," by Jessie Scanlon, Carolyn Rauch, David Jang (January), pp. 18–19.

Domus — "Guggenheim Virtual Museum," by Hani Rashid (January), pp. 27–31.

Wired — "This is Your Life," (February), pp. 81–92.

Architecture — "Computer Power," Cathy Lang Ho (May), pp. 156–61.

The Stadium — "The Architecture of Mass Sport," (Dodger Stadium) (Rotterdam: NAI Publishers), p. 174.

Business Week — "Architectural Visions, the Airborne HQ," by Bruce Nussbaum (August 21–28), pp. 162–64.

New Flatness — Surface Tension in Digital Architecture. Book by Alicia Imperiale (Basel: Birkauser), pp. 64–65.

Architectura (AC) — "El Liquido Elemento," by Humberto Viccina (May–June), Peru, pp. 43–53.

New York — "Liquid Assets," by Joseph Giovaninni (September 11), pp. 189, 223.

New Architecture 5 — "Virtual Guggenheim," Asymptote (No. 5), London, pp. 118–19.

The New York Times — "Three-Dimensional Space Is the Next Frontier for the Internet," by Matthew Mirapaul (Oct. 5, 2000, Circuits section).

Form — "Architekten i Cyberland," by Leo Gullbring (March), Stockholm, pp. 42–47.

40 Architects Under 40 — "Asymptote," by Jessica Cargill Thompson (Cologne: Taschen), pp. 82–91.

Arch+ — "Iscapes 1.0," by Ruth Berktold (October), pp. 102-3.

Prototypo — "Time Capsules," Asymptote (November), Lisbon.

Vision og Virkelighed — "Hani Rashid od Lise Anne Couture," by Berit Anne Larsen (Copenhagen: Louisiana Museum of Modern Art), pp. 76–77.

A+U — "Guggenheim Virtual," (January), p. 105.

Less Aesthetics More Ethics — Exhibition catalogue, La Biennale di Venezia (Venice: Marsilio Editori), pp. 164–67.

Zoo — (Issue 6, August), UK, p. 106.

1999

Big — "Futurespace, Digital Images: Asymptote Architecture" (Issue 24), New York, pp. 62–67.

Understanding USA — "Hani Rashid/Lise Anne Couture," by Richard Saul Wurman. Proceedings from 10th TedX conference, Monterey, California.

Prototypo 001 — "The Difference-Scape: The Digital Machine," Lisbon, pp. 122–37.

The Art of the Accident — "The Difference-Scape." Dutch Electronic Art Festival (Rotterdam: NAi Publishers), pp. 35, 37.

A+U — "Asymptote, Rashid und Couture," (No. 344, May), Tokyo, pp. 22–37.

ArchiLab Orleans '99 — Exhibition catalogue (Orleans, France: Archilab), pp. 34–41.

Wired — "Ride the Dow," by Jessie Scanlo (June), pp. 176–79.

Surface — "New Guggenheim," by Marisa S. Olson (No. 18), pp. 40–41.

Domus — "The Advanced Trading Floor Operation Center in the NYSE," (June), pp. 39–46.

Architectural Record — "Asymptote's Dual Projects for the NYSE," by Sarah Amelar (June), pp. 140–45.

Interview — "Thirty to Watch," by Richard Pandiscio (October), pp. 150–54.

Parachute — "The Architecture of Convergences," (No. 96), Montreal, pp. 59–61.

	Esquire	"The Esquire 21," Genius Issue (November), pp. 123, 130–31.
	Artbyte	"Asymptote Iscapes," by Kevin Pratt (Nov./Dec.), pp. 64–69.
	Time	"Leaders for the 21st Century," by Sandy Fernandez (September 27, 1999), Canada, p. 80.
	Architectural Record	"The Millenium: Futures to Come," by Kurt Anderson (December), pp. 85–87, 92–95.
	Casabella	"Asymptote Architecture," edited by Nicholas Adams and Joan Ockman (December), pp. 107–11.
	Guggenheim	"Guggenheim Virtual Museum," Matthew Drutt (Fall) (New York: Solomon R. Guggenheim Museum).
1998	TransArchitectures 03	Exhibition catalogue (Berlin: Aedes Galerie), p. 16.
	Hypersurface Architecture	AD Profile No. 133, by Stephen Perella (London: Architectural Design), pp. 62, 65.
	Korean Architect (KA)	"Asymptote," (June), Seoul, pp. 36–63.
	The Virtual Dimension	"The Difference-Scape." Book by John Beckman (New York: Princeton Architectural Press), pp. 286–91.
1997	The Berlage Cahiers Catalogue	"Texturing Amsterdam," (Rotterdam: The Berlage Institute), pp. 50–53.
	A+U	"Univers Theatre," (No. 323), Tokyo, pp.10–23.
	Architecti	"Teatro Univers, Aarhus Dinmarca," (No. 37, May/June), Lisbon, pp. 18–29.
	World Architecture	"Designing the Unpredictable," by Georgi Stanishev (No. 54, March), London, pp. 72–75.
	Arkitekten	"Dynamisk Bybygning," by Morten Daugaard (Vol. 33), Copenhagen, pp. 10–13.
	Architecture	"Dream Machine," by Aaron Betsky (June), pp. 88–91.
1996	Architectural Profile	"Architexturing Copenhagen," (Vol. 1), Bangkok, pp. 14, 12–19.
	Den Oversete	"Arkitecktur/Architecture," (December), Copenhagen, p. 153.
	Paper Art 6	Edited by Dorothea Eimert. Leopold-Hoesch-Museum, Duren, Germany (Stuttgart: Cantz Verlag), pp. 116–19.
	Fifty-One World Architects	"Crosscurrents." Book edited by Masayuki Fuchigami (Tokyo: Synectics Inc.), pp. 138–41.
	Columbia Documents	"Ceci N'est Pas un Building." (New York: Columbia University), pp. 23–41.
	Studio Art Magazine	"On Flickers and Solid," by Yar Milet and Aleksandra Wagner (No. 76–82), Tel Aviv.
	BAU014	"Museo Historico de Tohuku/Arquitexturas en Copenhague," (Vol. 14), Madrid, pp. 12–19.
	Die Schrift des Raumes	"Kunst Architecture Kunst." Catalog (Vienna: Kunstalle), pp. 16–17.
1995	Space: Arts and Architecture	"Asymptote Architecture." (Vol. 5:331), Seoul, pp. 57–63.
	Exposé	"Instaurations de L'eventuel," by Frédéric Migayrou (Vol. 2) (Orleans, France: FRAC Centre) pp. 206–11.
	Asymptote: Architecture at the Interval	Book by Hani Rashid and Lise Anne Couture (New York: Rizzoli International Publications).
	40 Under 40	Book edited by Beverly Russell (Grand Rapids, Missouri: Rockport), pp. 194–95.
	Architectura	"Steel Cloud." (Sept.), Mexico, pp. 32–33.
1994	A+U	"Asymptote." (April), Tokyo, pp. 47–139.
	Arkitekten	"Byen Under Foranding," by Morten Daugaard (July), Copenhagen, pp. 336–37.
	Urban Revisions	Catalogue edited by Elizabeth Smith and Russell Ferguson (Los Angeles: MOCA), pp. 84, 152–57.
	Architecture and Film	"Film as Architecture as Film" (Rashid and Couture). AD Profile No. 112 (London: Academy Editions), pp. 62–67.
1993	Metropolis	"Berlin Searches for Itself," by Sarah Amelar (December), pp. 42–45.
	Assemblage 21	"Analog Space to Digital Field: Asymptote Seven Projects." (Cambrige, Mass.: The MIT Press), pp. 22–43.
	Eciffo	"Aggressive Offices Created by World Architects." (Vol. 22, Autumn issue), Tokyo, pp. 4–7.
	Theory & Experimentation	"Asymptote." AD Profile No. 100 (London: Academy Editions), pp. 48, 110–19.
1992	Arquitectura	"Teatro Estatal de Moscu." (No. 6), Mexico City, pp. 46–47.
	L'Arca	"Nube d'acciaio," by Alessandro Gubitosi (No. 66, December), Milan, pp. 74–79.
	The New York Times	"Time to Reset the Clock in Times Square," by Herbert Muschamp (Nov. 1, 1992, Arts & Leisure section).
	SD-Space Design	(No. 336, September), Tokyo, pp. 62–67.
1991	AD Profile	"Optigraphs and Other Writings," by Hani Rashid. AD Profile No. 89 (London: Academy Editions), pp. 86–91.
	New Spirit in Architecture	Edited by Peter Cook and Rosie Liewellyn-Jones. (New York: Rizzoli International Publications), pp. 132–35.
	Technique & Architecture	(No. 394), Paris, pp. 102–5.
	Archithese	(Jan.–Feb.), Zurich, pp. 74–5.
1990	Deconstruction III	AD Profile No. 87 (London: Academy Editions), pp. 52, 58, 61.
	A+U	"Lebbeus Woods, RIEA and its Berlin Exhibition of Experimental Architecture," (No. 241), Tokyo, pp. 38–39.
	Arkkitehti	"Deconstruction of a Monument," by Juhani Pallasmaa, Helsinki, pp. 70–83.
1989	Paris: Architecture and Utopia	"On Recent Non-Events." Catalogue edited by Kristen Feireiss. (Paris: City of Paris, Pavilion d'Arsenal), pp. 166-7.
	A+U	"Hani Rashid and Lise Anne Couture," (No. 231, December), Tokyo, pp. 5–28.
	Interiors	"30 Under 30," (September), pp. 166–71.
	Artforum International	"Ground Up," by Herbert Muschamp (Vol. 28, No. 1).
	Plus	(No. 23, March), Seoul, pp. 154–9.
	Skala	"West Coast Gateway," by Kate Nesbitt (No. 17/18), Copenhagen, pp. 28–9.

Phaidon Press Limited
Regent's Wharf
All Saints Street
London N1 9PA

Phaidon Press Inc.
180 Varick Street
New York, NY 10014

www.phaidon.com

First published 2002
© 2002 Phaidon Press Limited

ISBN 0 7148 4172 2

A CIP catalogue record of this book is available from the British Library.

Designed by Hannah Yampolsky | Asymptote

Printed in China

All graphics and photos courtesy of Asymptote unless otherwise noted.